The User's View of the Internet

Harry Bruce

The Scarecrow Press, Inc.
Lanham, Maryland, and London
2002

SCARECROW PRESS, INC.

Published in the United States of America
by Scarecrow Press, Inc.
A Member of the Rowman & Littlefield Publishing Group
4720 Boston Way, Lanham, Maryland 20706
www.scarecrowpress.com

4 Pleydell Gardens, Folkestone
Kent CT20 2DN, England

British Library Cataloguing-in-Publication Information Available

Library of Congress Cataloging-in-Publication Data

Bruce, Harry, 1957–
  The user's view of the Internet / Harry Bruce.
       p. cm.
Includes bibliographical references and index.
  ISBN 0-8108-4365-X (cloth)—ISBN 0-8108-4366-8 (paper)
  1. Internet. 2. Research. 3. Internet users. I. Title.
  TK5105.875.I57 .B7623 2002
  004.67'8—dc21

                                                    2002003114

⊖™ The paper used in this publication meets the minimum requirements of
American National Standard for Information Sciences—Permanence of
Paper for Printed Library Materials, ANSI/NISO Z39.48-1992.
Manufactured in the United States of America.

To Lorraine, Sarah, and Caitlin

Contents

Preface

The User's View of the Internet is a composite of ideas and reflections emerging from ten years of research and observation. My interest in the Internet began in 1992 when I attended a Networkshop Conference in Hobart, Australia. During the late 1980s, communication and computer engineers from universities around Australia met at Networkshop conferences to facilitate the development of the Australian Academic and Research Network. AARNet was officially launched in 1990, giving Australian academics and researchers access to the Internet. I had been asked to attend the Networkshop Conference to find out about AARNet and to assess how it might be used by academics in my school. I was immediately struck by the potential of the Internet to transform the way I was working as a researcher and teacher. I assumed that the people who were using the network were deriving enormous benefit from this new way of communicating and finding and transferring information. It was with some surprise that I overheard a program organizer comment on the last day of the event that it would be a great idea to invite some users to the next Networkshop conference to find out how and why people in the Australian academic community were using the AARNet.

My field is information science. At that time, I was working in an Information School at the University of Technology in Sydney. The professional programs, teaching, and research of academics and students in this school were based on the user-oriented paradigm. This conceptual framework places the user at the center of all considerations related to the design and implementation of information systems and services. Equivalent frameworks are found in a number of other fields. It seemed strange, therefore, that the complex and expensive infrastructures of the Internet could have been established without some preliminary or even concurrent study of the people who would be using the network. Investigating this further, I discovered that researchers like McClure in the United States were trying to address this issue but that many of the claims being made about the benefits of using the Internet—and the rhetoric at the time was substantial—were largely untested. This launched my research program which spanned the following decade and comprised five research projects aimed at enhancing our understanding of how and why people are using the Internet.

My research was conducted during the 1990s, when using the Internet became commonplace. The people in my studies, academics and affiliated users, are no longer the primary users of the Internet. During the 1990s, the general public or everyday user emerged and Internet technologies developed in response to demands by people who wanted to find information and communicate with others on the network. The Internet developed along what I refer to as *using trajectories*. The network and its services evolved from using. It grew in directions, and was innovated in ways, that accommodated how people wanted to use the network. Because of the rapid pace of these transformations, it is difficult to know if demand preceded innovation in all cases but, as the numbers of people using the Internet increased exponentially through this period, the Internet became easier to use. The story of the Internet in the 1990s, therefore, is about technology innovation and adoption by people on a very large scale.

With the emergence of widespread use of the Internet in the 1990s, various stakeholders and service providers began to see the everyday users of the network as potential customers, clients, constituents, audiences, learners, beneficiaries of service, and so on. Understanding what people want to do and how they want to use the network became very important, and many Internet user studies were conducted. This research activity across the middle of the decade encouraged me to publish a number of articles that analyzed the common conceptualization of the Internet as an information infrastructure. My analysis drew attention to how user centered definitions of the concept "information" within the term "information infrastructure" could be used to promote and reinforce certain qualities of the Internet. There seemed to be a piece of the puzzle missing, however. These studies revealed that we can understand how and why people are using the Internet and we can use these findings to inform the design of new services and to augment our using of the Internet. But how at a metatheoretical level was user oriented research helping us to understand the phenomenon of the Internet?

This question led me back to the work of Brenda Dervin who, in the late 1990s, was expressing some doubt about our focus on users per se. Rather, she claimed, we should be attentive to micromoments of using—the mini events in peoples' lives that weave together information, contexts, and systems. Instead of focusing on users, we should be focused on usings. This made a great deal of sense to me but it was not until I connected Dervin's views with the work of Latour that I found the explanation I was looking for. My merging of Dervin and Latour, explains how the study of Internet usings builds our understanding of the Internet phenomenon.

Given this refined theoretical lens and the data from numerous studies of people using the Internet—what do we know about the network and the people who are using it? *The User's View of the Internet* provides a theoretical model and a set of propositions for stakeholders to consider.

Most authors reach a point in their intellectual journey when they would like to invite others to join them. To explain what we think to others, we need to unravel and then reassemble the components of our insight—to create the paths that we want our readers to travel. With *The User's View of the Internet*, I hope my readers will recognize themselves and see their clients, audiences, students, or users in a new light. I hope my readers will be able to apply these enhanced perceptions to the improvement, augmentation, or design of services, and in this way, I trust that the story of the Internet and our understanding of the Internet

Acknowledgments

The writing of this book required the assistance of many people. I would like to thank Mike Eisenberg, who helped me find a publisher. I would like to thank Catherine Stickley for her meticulous attention to detail, superb research skills, and for coordinating many of the writing and publishing activities associated with the preparation of this manuscript. I would also like to thank John Stickley who produced the graphic representations for *The User's View of the Internet* that appear in chapter 5. Finally, I would like to thank Kim Prater for completing the copyediting corrections to the manuscript and for preparing the book's index.

Chapter 1

The Internet Story

The Internet is a complex web of interconnected local and national computer networks. This network of networks connects people with myriad computer-based information products, resources, and services. It facilitates the dissemination of new knowledge generated by research and scholarship. It helps governments inform their constituents. It connects developers and innovators with customers and clients. It connects people who are seeking affiliation and affirmation.

The Internet has been characterized and popularized by terms such as information superhighway, Infobahn, global network, and information infrastructure.[1] In truth, it has become a new frontier where people are challenged to think differently about information and knowledge, teaching and learning, new media and publishing, public policy, commercial services, and business.

The story of the Internet is a story about research, technology and innovation, information, and communication. But most of all, the Internet is a story about people. It is about the people who conceived the technologies of internetworking and who valued collaboration and sharing and saw in first-generation computing devices the potential to transform the way humans make contact, collaborate, communicate, and find information. The real story of the Internet is not about the Internet. It is about people sharing information and searching for information or for other people. It is the story of people developing new resources and services. It is about people publishing and disseminating new ideas. It is about people investing in a public infrastructure with a vision for universal access to information. It is about people doing their job and promoting professional values with new and improved tools. It is about people developing new ways to do business and to serve others. It is about people buying and selling things. It is about people learning and teaching. It is about people taking risks and making choices and decisions. It is a story about innovative and creative thinkers and the ideas and values of individuals and groups of people.

At the dawn of the twenty-first century, the Internet, for the people of modern industrialized societies at least, is becoming ubiquitous. The story of the Internet has, therefore, become the story of applications and uses by the general public—the story of end users. This book elaborates the user perspective or user view. It describes the users of the Internet through research into the uses and usings of the network by people. It answers the question, "What is the Internet?" by focusing on *who* the Internet is. It tells the story of the end-user provenance of the Internet and the story of developments, applications, and innovations that have been driven by the character of Internet use and using.

The book begins with the story of Internet evolution. When we use the metaphor of a technology evolving, what do we mean and what do we imply about the characteristics of the technology? We suggest that it is growing, developing, changing, and transforming in response to the environment. It is surviving through hybridization. Parts that are unused grow no bigger, die or wither. Parts that are well used prosper and grow. Development and survival are ruled by use and using. Where there is no use, development stops. Where there is the need for use or different types of using, development responds with applications and innovations.

Use and using for the Internet are like light to a plant. A plant will grow in the direction of a light source. This is true for the Internet and its evolution. As the Internet developed, people began to use it and to make demands for innovation. They indicated the sorts of information sources, resources, and services they wanted to share, how they wanted to access these resources, and what types of interfaces they wanted to use and how difficult or easy they wanted these interfaces to be. The trajectories of Internet development followed the pathways of these user demands.

The stakeholders in Internet development are also use and using driven. The stakeholders who are the featured audience for this book are Internet users, but they also serve individual users and user communities. They include industries and professional fields that observe, use, and attempt to respond to what people want to do on the Internet. These stakeholders also engage in professional practices that are underpinned by models and values that are oriented toward people or users. The analysis presented in this book serves a theoretical framework that emerged from contemporary social and psychological imperatives that focus upon the individual. We call this framework the user-oriented paradigm. The period in which the Internet developed, and indeed continues to develop, coincides with the emergence of theoretical frameworks that center on people who value service, design products according to need, target clients rather than markets, and focus on learning rather than teaching or educational institutions.

The development of the Internet is also the story of the development of technology on a grand scale. This aspect of the story taught us the value and importance of computing and of geeks. It is a story that expresses the creativity of people. The development of the Internet is a story of technological innovation and diffusion. It is a story of people from many backgrounds accepting and promoting rhetoric, values, and benefits. It is the story of people investing in a technology with a widely accepted potential for good—a technology predicted to change the way people collaborate, work, publish, research, teach, communicate, and find information. This technology was installed and implemented before the validity of the claim to these outcomes could be rigorously tested or evaluated, so the story of the Internet is also the story of a rhetoric that developed its own momentum and powers to persuade people. It is the story of people in political office, boards of directors, educational administrators, and venture capitalists who accepted the predictions of benefit, value, and profit and invested large sums of money on the assumption that the Internet would transform our lives.

So we can see, at every turn of this story, people are involved. People are the catalyzers, the justification, and the market. People are the groundswell. People are the reason and the driving force. People are the champions and the detractors. People are the users and developers. And as the story of the Internet continues, it will be told through the actions and thoughts of people. It is impossible to predict the exact form that the Internet will take in the future but we will certainly not talk about the Internet the way we do today—as a tangible entity. As the Internet becomes increasingly ubiquitous, we will pay less attention to the novelty of the infrastructure and more to the applications and services that support the way people want to use the network. In the future, the Internet will be more about people than it is today. It will continue to tell the story of people and their involvement with information and with one another. It will be about how people are transforming our notions of teaching and learning, information seeking and gathering, publication and dissemination, business transactions, and other uses that we haven't yet imagined. The user's view of the Internet will continue to be the most effective lens for analyzing, evaluating, and understanding this modern phenomenon.

The Evolution of the Internet

Internet is a shortening of the term *internetworking*. This term simply describes the interconnection of similar and dissimilar networks. The protocols that facilitate internetworking are the outcome of over twenty years of research and innovation in computer communications technology,[2] emerging in the first instance from a technological think tank of the Department of Defense. The Advanced Research Projects Agency (ARPA) was formed in reaction to the launching of Sputnik by the USSR in

October 1957. In fact, some say that ARPA would not have happened if the blow to U.S. confidence resulting from the launching of Sputnik had not occurred.[3] The activities of the research agency were initially focused on space exploration and nuclear testing. Eventually, however, advanced computing and networks would dominate the research programs of ARPA.

In the early 1960s computers were huge machines locked in rooms and accessible to few human beings other than a small number of highly specialized data processing professionals. It may seem unlikely that these technologies could provoke the attention of a behavioral sciences division of ARPA. Nonetheless, at this time, the Information Processing Techniques Office (IPTO), headed by J. R. Licklider, a psycho-acoustician, began to investigate different approaches to computing including graphics, communications, and educational applications. During the 1950s, while employed by Bolt Beranek Newman, Licklider had been able to explore the relationship that a person might have with a computer and had promoted the idea of a man-machine interface. When he was appointed head of IPTO in 1961, he published a memorandum on the concept of a Galactic Network concept that was futuristic in its vision of computers networked together and accessible to everyone.[4]

Others were also thinking about different approaches to computing at this time. One of these individuals was Bob Taylor. In 1961, Taylor, an experimental psychologist, was NASA's representative on a project hosted by the Stanford Research Institute that was looking for better ways for human beings to interact with and use computers. An innovative way of thinking about people using computers that emerged at this time was the concept of time-sharing. Rather than having expensive mainframe computers devoted to serving the needs of a single person at a time, time-sharing introduced the idea that computer processing power could be shared among a number of users. At the beginning of the 1960s this was quite a revolution in thinking about the human and computer. In its early form, time-sharing provided the computer user with a first version of individual desktop computing.

The computer user served by time-sharing was an elite, technically savvy graduate student or computer engineer. From this user's perspective, time-sharing was a great advance. The individual user now had direct access to the processing power of the computer via a terminal rather than waiting for a data processing professional to punch in his or her program and then waiting perhaps days for the results. The subculture of the computer "hacker" emerged from this first computer user group as did the counterculture of egalitarianism and sharing which later manifested itself through the evolution of the Internet. In fact, it was this first group of computer users who conceived of, and developed ways of, using the computer for communicating with one another. Email grew out of the hacker culture, as did the imperative to find effective ways of communicating with fellow users.

Taylor at IPTO saw the usefulness of time-sharing but was deeply frustrated by the fact that he could only communicate with people who were sharing the same system. In order to communicate with people using another system, he had to go to a terminal attached to that other system. Taylor concluded that there had to be way of sending messages between systems so he convinced the head of ARPA, Charles Hertzfeld, to assign a million dollars of funding to explore this concept.[5] The vision of interconnected computer systems was born as the ARPANET.

The program manager assigned to the ARPANET project was Larry Roberts. Roberts found the solution to the problem of moving data back and forth between networks in a construction first postulated in 1956 by Paul Baran of the Rand Corporation. Baran had formulated the idea of *packets* of data moving between computer systems. ARPANET became a research project exploring this concept of packet switching.

The technique of packet switching sends messages or data in individually addressed packets. For longer messages, the content is broken down and sent as a sequence of packets. The technology allows packets from different communication sessions to be interspersed on the same line. In the event of equipment failure, packets can be rerouted with no effect on the communications session.[6]

The success of packet switching as a concept thus relied upon the technology that would move and direct (route) packets of data through a network. For a short time, ARPA researchers thought that the solution to this lay in each host or main computer of a system being able to talk to all the computers in other systems. Wes Clark of Washington University in St. Louis proposed an alternative to this idea. Clark suggested the design of a new computer with two functions. First, it would pass data packets around the ARPANET, and second, it would translate data packets that were addressed to people on the constituent network to which it was attached so that the data packet had the same format as the computers used in its network. This technology is now called a *router*.[7]

ARPANET routers were called interface message processors (IMPs). The host computers of ARPANET were connected directly to an IMP. Many IMPs were linked to more than one computer. The number of IMPs quickly grew from 10 in mid-1970 to roughly 100 by the early 1980s.[8]

As a prototype packet switching network, ARPANET was regarded as highly successful.[9] It became an economically viable service utility for the computer science research community. Much of the driving force behind this success was the insistence by Taylor that all IPTO and ARPA grant recipients must join the network. Taylor's strategy established the first group of users (people working mainly in academic and government agencies) committed to the value of internetworking. The more these researchers used the network, the more convinced they became of the benefits derived from the enhanced communication that the network provided. Researchers quickly developed messaging programs that became known as *email*. Newsgroups and bulletin boards were established allowing these scientists and researchers to share information. This experimental network provided its first users with tools that enhanced communication, affiliation, and the dissemination of ideas but it was also an economic success. It was estimated in 1973, for example, that the ARPANET saved approximately $4 million by simply avoiding duplication of resources by the U.S. research community. More important, ARPANET served its users by providing the context for network research that ultimately facilitated the creation of the protocols needed for internetworking.[10]

Up to the mid-1970s, ARPANET functioned on a Network Control Program (NCP) protocol. This protocol was inflexible because it was host based. It operated only within the communications subnet created by the interface message processors of the ARPANET. In 1981, the NCP protocol was replaced by the Transmission Control Protocol (TCP) and Internet Protocol (IP). The key authors of TCP/IP were Steve Crocker, Bob Kahn, and Vinton Cerf of UCLA. These communications protocols, used in conjunction with one another, underpin the interconnectivity upon which a network of networks relies. They work through devices called *gateways*, which use the TCP/IP protocols to convert a message from the language of one network to that of another.[11] TCP/IP was developed to run on any operating system, allowing disparate computers to join the network.

Within the TCP/IP protocol suite, there are three main computer communications protocols, which tend to be implemented on all computers on the network. These three protocols formed the basis for computer-to-computer communications throughout the Internet. They are the Simple Mail Transfer Protocol (SMTP), which supports electronic mail; the File Transfer Protocol (FTP), which supports file transfer from one computer to another; and the Telnet Session Protocol (TSP), which supports terminal sessions to remote computers.[12]

The ability to send and receive data between heterogeneous and homogeneous networks, which the TCP/IP suite provided, established the technological framework for internetworking. There are several requirements for internetworking. These are a

consistent form of internet addressing—to enable communications between users on the various constituent subnetworks; points of interconnection between the networks; a mechanism to route and control the flow of information on the internet; and common protocols at some level in order to enable different constituent networks to communicate with each other.[13]

TCP provided the standard way for computers to share network traffic. IP provided the way that packets of data could be addressed and delivered.

Adoption of TCP/IP by ARPANET gave rise to a gradual redefinition of internetwork users. At this time, control of ARPA passed to the Defense Communications Agency and then to the National Science Foundation. In this way, use of the network shifted from defense contractors to widespread use by the academic community. In fact, the explicit requirement for receiving funding for connection to what was now called the NSFNet was that access had to be provided for all qualified users on a campus. This trend was also occurring in other parts of the world, where national governments were encouraging the use of internetworked computer systems by the higher education sector. In 1984, for example, the British government sponsored the Joint Academic Network (JANET) to serve British universities. At the same time, the variety of academic disciplines and fields using these networks was widening to include scholars working in the humanities and social sciences and other fields as well as computer science and engineering faculty and students.

The protocols that were developed by the ARPANET testbed in the early 1980s have underpinned the subsequent development of internetworking in many countries throughout the world. The term *Internet* is now commonly used to identify an international wide area network which links the computers of local area networks in research, educational, military, and commercial organizations around the world.[14] The Internet links NSFNet in the United States to other TCP/IP networks such as JANET in the United Kingdom, NORDUNet in Scandinavia, JUNET in Japan,[15] FUNET in Finland, RedIRIS in Spain, SURFnet in the Netherlands,[16] and AARNet in Australia.

The network became an accumulation of interconnected sites. Widespread adoption of TCP/IP meant that each constituent network only needed a router in order to connect with other and even dissimilar networks. In a sense, the Internet is really a collection of routers that talk the same language and pass data back and forth. By 1983, the concept of an *Internet* of interconnected networks had become widely accepted.

One of the important nodes to the Internet at this time was the European Laboratory for Particle Physics (*Conseil Européen pour la Recherche Nucleaire,* or CERN). The CERN laboratory represented a significant group of Internet users (about 9,000 physicists) who had particular needs related to data sharing and communication that were as yet unmet or ill-served by the fledgling Internet. These scientists wanted to share photographs and graphics related to research and development in the field of physics. A programmer named Tim Berners-Lee provided the solution to their problem.[17]

Berners-Lee had been toying with the idea of creating a set of interlinked and interconnected electronic documents since he started work as a graduate student at CERN in 1979. He called the set of documents a Web and coined the term "World Wide Web" to describe his vision of interconnected and interrelated pieces of digital information. By 1990, this idea was not quite so far-fetched and the programmer created a prototype of a handful of pages of an electronic document that he could navigate using a *browser.* This program was distributed by CERN to other members of the Internet user community (mainly students, members of the academic sector, and computer and communications engineers). It did not take long for members of this community to realize the potential of Berners-Lee's idea.

At this time, Berners-Lee had no real interest in the transmission of graphics over the Internet, but others did. Dave Thompson at the National Center for Supercomputer Applications (NCSA) at the University of Illinois in Champaign recognized the needs of the thousands of computer scientists who used NCSA services across the Internet. Thompson obtained a copy of Berners-Lee's program and showed it to Marc Andreessen. Andreessen began the process of creating an NCSA version of the CERN browser. To achieve this, Andreessen sought the assistance of a superstar programmer working at NCSA named Eric Bina. In six weeks, the two had created the browser known as Mosaic.[18]

The breakthrough that Bina made with the development of Mosaic relates to his anticipation of what unsophisticated Internet users would like to be able to do. He recognized that the contemporary general-purpose computer applications that people were using in their homes and offices allowed the user to point and click when he or she wanted the application to function. The unsophisticated user expected to be able to do the same thing when connected to the Internet. Most general-purpose application software also integrated text and graphics, and Bina realized that the unsophisticated Internet user would also expect to see graphics and that Web page developers should be responding to this expectation and browsers should be capable of allowing the user to view all elements of the website design.

In 1993, NCSA distributed Mosaic free of charge to the Internet community, making the Internet much more usable and paving the way for a broader-based general public use of the network. Up to this point, users of the network had generally been associated with the academic or government sector—a middle-up infrastructure. NSCA's Mosaic made it possible for the Internet experiment to reach beyond this small group of elite, affiliated users.

At the same time as these design breakthroughs were occurring, the user base of the Internet was also gradually expanding and this was attracting the attention of communities outside the academic and government sector. Up to this time, businesses that wanted to use the Internet were denied access to the NSFNet but in 1991, the National Science Foundation lifted this ban.[19] This breakthrough encouraged people with a business perspective to take a closer look at the Internet. Commercial imperatives and market forces were about to play a role in the innovation and diffusion of the network.

Marc Andreessen and Jim Clark of Silicon Graphics speculated that there was money to be made from a commercial version of Mosaic. In 1994, they formed the company that they called Netscape and by the end of the same year, the company was a hot success story. The company's success was based on giving away its browser free of charge. This meant that the Internet user profile began to change almost immediately. No longer was the network the exclusive domain of the academic and research community. With a browser, even unsophisticated, unaffiliated users could access the services of the Internet. This broader user base further encouraged businesses to seriously consider the Internet as a viable context for commercial transactions and market development.

It is difficult to gauge whether Netscape's strategy was the chicken or the egg in the sudden rise in Internet use through the 1990s. Either way, the company demonstrated that once enough people were using the Internet, the environment could be exploited for commercial advantage. The company confirmed that the Internet was the way of the future for business. In May 1995, the limitations to commercial use of the Internet were completely lifted when the NSF ended its sponsorship of the Internet backbone. All traffic across the Internet now relied on commercial networks.[20]

Of course, Netscape was not the only company to realize that internetworking was rapidly becoming the key infrastructure for information transfer and commercial transactions within and between modern economies. The phenomenal success of Netscape sent a clear message to Bill Gates, the CEO of Microsoft. Gates realized that his company's control of personal computing would depend on repositioning Microsoft toward the Internet. This process began in December 1995. Netscape's initial success established the paradigm for Internet innovation for the mid-1990s. Microsoft's actions in seizing upon this new paradigm and repositioning the company's product line and services are critical factors in the company's continued dominance of the information technology field. These actions in turn drew further public attention to the importance of the ongoing development of network technologies.

From its user provenance as a middle-up infrastructure designed to serve the interests of a select research community, the Internet has thus moved to the broad-based infrastructure that we see today. The network continues to be responsive to the market, social, and political forces that shape its development but at the heart of these imperatives are the values, creativity, intelligence, and will of the general public, communities, and society that derive benefit from Internet connectivity.

What Is the Internet?

As the Internet became more popular through the 1990s and the types of people using the Internet broadened, it was politically, culturally, and commercially expedient to insinuate the benefits derived from using network services through popular characterizations of the network. These characterizations drew public attention to the role that networked services might play in the lives of people. They also focused attention on social issues and political agendas that inevitably arise from a phenomenon as pervasive and compelling as the Internet.

The evolution of the Internet occurred during a period of time commonly characterized as the Information Age. During this period, modern developed countries began using the term *information society* to emphasize that information in these economies is a key factor in the success of organizations, institutions, governments, businesses, and individuals. It is not surprising, therefore, that the Internet was characterized and popularized in ways that take advantage of this view.

The term *information superhighway*, for example, originated from a speech given by Vice President Al Gore. In this speech, Gore was promoting the Clinton administration's plan to deregulate communication services. The term was used to characterize the Internet because it provided a hook for promoting the benefits of the Internet to a growing user base. The term emphasized the view that the Internet connected people to the information that they need.

The same is true for the term *information infrastructure*. Again, this term emerged from a political agenda but was quickly picked up as a way of describing the Internet. The term capitalized on the general understanding that information is of critical importance to people. The concept of an information infrastructure has several layers of meaning. The Agenda for Action which underpinned the National Information Infrastructure Act of 1993,[21] accepted an expansive definition which encompassed a wide range of equipment and types of information; applications and software that allow people to access, manipulate, and organize information and network standards and transmission codes that facilitate interconnection and interoperation among networks. At this time, Vinton Cerf defined *information infrastructure* as the common ground on which digital information products and services achieve interoperability.[22] Cerf included in his definition technical standards, communication services, and legal and regulatory frameworks.

From one perspective, then, an information infrastructure is an interoperable and open systems environment supporting a variety of applications that allow digital data to pass across networks and technologies. At this level, the technological characteristics of the Internet are accurately emphasized. But the concept of an information infrastructure is also explicitly associated with people, connectivity, and information access. When the term *information infrastructure* was coined and applied in the political sense, it also incorporated the notion of universal service—ensuring that the information resources and services on the Internet are universally available and affordable for people to use.[23] Within this characterization of the Internet resides the vision of universal access to distributed information resources and the benefits that this will bring to the lives of individual people and to society in general.

In 1995, the Federal Networking Council (FNC) promoted a definition of the Internet that integrated this notion of a connective infrastructure with the implied values of networked information and communication services. This definition is also interesting in light of the fact that it includes the view that the Internet is a medium for human creativity and innovation— perceiving the Internet as a medium where the human condition is manifest through communication, publication, affiliation, affirmation, and innovation. The FNC defined the Internet as a global information system that

> (i) is logically linked together by a globally unique address space based on the Internet Protocol (IP) of subsequent extensions/follow-ons;
> (ii) is able to support communications using the Transmission Control Protocol/Internet Protocol (TCP/IP) suite or its

subsequent extensions/follow-ons, and/or other IP-compatible protocols; and

(iii) provides, uses or makes accessible, either publicly or privately, high level services layered on the communication and related infrastructure described herein.[24]

In the broader vision of an information infrastructure (the Internet is the only model currently operational), we see a set of commonly accepted assumptions, which assign goodness and value to information processes, artifacts, products, and services. Among other things, we assume that good decisions arise from good information, good democracy is based on making information available to all sectors of society, and wisdom is the by-product of effective use of information. If the Internet is an information infrastructure, then the Internet is good and using the Internet will benefit individuals and society in general.

In the early stages of Internet development described earlier as an evolution, the good derived from the information transferred across the Internet came to a select group of people who were connected to the experimental network. The benefits that this select user community obtained were generally related to professional roles. Researchers would have access to information that they needed, collaboration between researchers would be facilitated, and the outcomes of research would be transferred quickly to the beneficiaries of this work and the scholarly community. As the user base for the Internet expanded, further professional benefits surfaced. Librarians realized that information provision in a networked environment provided extraordinary scope for enhancing traditional roles and expanding and transforming the functions of the library. Educators realized that the Internet provided opportunities to engage innovative pedagogies across diverse communities of learners. Businessmen and businesswomen realized that the broad user base of the Internet meant that they could connect with clients and markets around the globe. Governments realized that the Internet provided a mechanism for communicating with constituents, advocating policy, and delivering the services of public utilities.

One of the most intriguing things to emerge from the Internet story, however, is the extent to which the innovations associated with connectivity technologies have confused the professional and personal dimensions of our lives. We are increasingly connected, scheduled, and available. Our professional and personal, work and everyday, lives overlap. In this way, the professional benefits of using the Internet have transitioned into everyday personal uses of the Internet. The general public is discovering information and people on the Internet that have value to their personal as well as professional lives. They are discovering uses of the Internet such as personal development, electronic shopping, hobbies, recreation and games, music, publication, advocacy of individual causes and interests, communication with family and friends, and so on. These uses will continue to tell the story of Internet's development and further transformation and suggest that earlier constructions of the Internet as information infrastructure are now far too simplistic.

To date, we have sought characterizations for the Internet that serve political expediency and promote the rhetoric that has been critical to the development, funding, and promotion of the network. Our ongoing motivation for seeking characterizations of the Internet, however, is the need to develop a deeper level conceptual understanding of the role that it plays in the lives of people as individuals and members of professions and communities. How should we characterize the Internet as it continues to be transformed through trajectories of innovation that are stimulated by people using the network? The user provenance of the Internet is clear from the story told thus far. A better understanding of what will, or ought to, come next can be achieved by the deeper level understanding of the user's view of the Internet that we are seeking through the analysis presented in this book.

Notes

1. C. Arms, "A New Information Infrastructure," *Online* 14, no. 5 (1990); Vinton G. Cerf, "On National Information Infrastructure," *Bul-*

letin of the American Society for Information Science 20, no. 2 (1994); Vinton G. Cerf, "Some Possible Government Roles in Information Infrastructure," *Serials Review* 21, no. 1 (1995); L. Dempsey, "Research Networks and Academic Information Services: Towards an Academic Infrastructure: Part 1," *Journal of Information Networking* 1, no. 1 (1993); B. Kahin, "Information Technology and Information Infrastructure," in *Empowering Technology: Implementing a U.S. Strategy*, ed. L. M. Branscomb (Cambridge, Mass.: MIT Press, 1993); B. Kahin, "The Internet and the National Information Infrastructure," in *Public Access to the Internet*, ed. B. Kahin and J. Keller (Cambridge, Mass.: MIT Press, 1995); Clifford A. Lynch and Cecilia M. Preston, "Internet Access to Information Resources," in *Annual Review of Information Science and Technology*, ed. Martha E. Williams (Amsterdam: Elsevier Science Publishers, 1990); United States Department of Commerce, Information Infrastructure Taskforce, *National Information Infrastructure: Agenda for Action* (Washington, D.C.: United States Department of Commerce, Information Infrastructure Taskforce, 1993).

2. C. A. Lynch and C. M. Preston, "Evolution of Networked Information Resources" (paper presented at the 12th National Online Meeting, New York, May 7-9, 1991).

3. Gregory R. Gromov, "History of the Internet and WWW: The Roads and Crossroads of Internet History," *Internet Valley*, http://www.internetvalley.com/intval.html, 2000 [accessed 24 March 2000].

4. Robert H. Zakon, "Hobbes Internet Timeline V5.0,", http://www.zakon.org/robert/internet/timeline/, 2000 [accessed 17 March 2000].

5. Jeffrey S. Young, *Forbes Greatest Technology Stories: Inspiring Tales of the Entrepreneurs and Inventors Who Revolutionized Modern Business* (New York: John Wiley & Sons, 1998).

6. Arms, "A New Information Infrastructure."

7. Young, *Forbes Greatest Technology Stories.*

8. Lynch and Preston, "Internet Access to Information Resources."

9. Arms, "A New Information Infrastructure."

10. Lynch and Preston, "Internet Access to Information Resources."

11. R. A. Corbin, "The Development of the National Research and Education Network," *Information Technology and Libraries* 10, no. 3 (1991).

12. Arms, "A New Information Infrastructure"; L. J. Kosmin, "Library Reference Resources: The Internet Challenge" (paper presented

at Online Information 1991, London, December 10-12, 1991); Lynch and Preston, "Evolution of Networked Information Resources."

13. L. L. Learn, "Networks: A Review of Their Technology, Architecture, and Implementation," *Library Hi Tech* 6, no. 2 (1988): 43.

14. M. Giguere, "An Introduction to Services Accessible on the Internet," *Education Libraries* 16, no. 2 (1992).

15. Arms, "A New Information Infrastructure."

16. Dempsey, "Research Networks and Academic Information Services."

17. Young, *Forbes Greatest Technology Stories*.

18. Young, *Forbes Greatest Technology Stories*.

19. Cochran Entertainment, "PBS Life on the Internet: Timeline," PBS, http://www.pbs.org/internet/timeline/timeline-txt.html, 1997 [accessed 24 March 2000].

20. Walt Howe, "A Brief History of the Internet," *Walt Howe's Internet Learning Center*, http://www.walthowe.com/navnet/history.html, 2001 [accessed 27 July 2001].

21. United States Department of Commerce, Information Infrastructure Taskforce, *National Information Infrastructure*.

22. Cerf, "Some Possible Government Roles in Information Infrastructure."

23. Kahin, "The Internet and the National Information Infrastructure."

24. United States Federal Networking Council, "Federal Networking Council Resolution: Definition of 'Internet,'" National Coordination Office for Information Technology Research and Development, Federal Networking Council, http://www.itrd.gov/fnc/Internet_res.html, 30 October 1995 [accessed 2 July 2001].

Chapter 2

Technology and People

The evolution of the Internet is a story of radical technological change and diffusion on a large scale. Over the course of time, the Internet became a national and then international framework for technological innovation. Innovations tend to follow technological trajectories[1] or vectors,[2] but the shape and character of these development agendas is a function of people using (adopting and adapting) the technology. In the case of Internet development, we have seen (and this will be reinforced in later chapters) that network innovations are evolving through demands that are placed on Internet services by people in the workplace and everyday life. To understand the Internet more deeply, we need to understand the relationship between people, innovation, and diffusion because technological change is basically a gradual and cumulative learning process. It is important therefore to understand the Internet in relation to the existing knowledge, attitudes, and beliefs of people who are using the network and its technologies.

Technology Acceptance

Diffusion of innovations occurs out of the cumulative decisions of individuals to accept and use a technology.[3] There has been a lot written in our technological age about the acceptance and adoption of technologies by individuals and why some accept and others reject technological innovation. Some writers have examined the determinants of information technology acceptance,[4] and others have focused on developing theoretical models for technology acceptance. A model of particular interest to the user's view of the Internet is the theoretical construct called *personal innovativeness*.[5] This construct identifies individuals who are likely to adopt innovations earlier than others and also serve as the opinion leaders and change agents so necessary for wider technology acceptance and diffusion. Personal innovativeness has played a central role in the evolution of the Internet and requires further elaboration, but before doing so, we should introduce some of the other theories that help us to explain the acceptance and use of technology by people.

One such theory, the *Theory of the Diffusion of Innovations,*[6] takes an information-centric view of technology acceptance by individuals and identifies a series of steps that people follow when adopting a new innovation: knowledge, persuasion, decision, implementation, and confirmation.[7] It is important to note that adopters are seen as situated in social systems where information about innovation flows and they perceive this information and then drive innovation adoption decisions. In this theory, there are five attributes of innovations that are perceived by individuals and ultimately influence adoption:

> *Relative advantage:* the degree to which an innovation is perceived as being better than its precursor
> *Compatibility:* the degree to which an innovation is perceived as being consistent with the existing values, and past experiences of potential adopters
> *Complexity:* the degree to which an innovation is perceived as being difficult to use
> *Observability:* the degree to which the results of an innovation are observable to others; and
> *Trialability:* the degree to which an innovation may be experimented with before adoption.[8]

Over time, the Theory of the Diffusion of Innovations has been validated[9] and augmented[10] so that the construct now includes:

> *Image:* the degree to which use of an innovation is perceived to enhance one's image or status in one's social system; and *Voluntariness of use:* the degree to which use of the innovation is perceived as being voluntary or of free will.[11]

There is some evidence that these innovation characteristics have played a role in the adoption of the Internet and Internet technologies by people in workplace settings. An instance of the influence of image, for example, is shown by data emerging from research that reveal academic faculty adopting and using the Internet because they see this as a professional obligation.[12] Voluntariness of use has also been identified as a characteristic of Internet adoption by academic faculty. Increased use of the Internet in the academic setting has tended to be as much an outcome of the wider adoption of this technology within a school, department, or university, as opposed to the personal endorsement and diffusion of Internet use by individual faculty.[13]

Recent augmentations of the Theory of the Diffusion of Innovations emphasize that the earlier construct was based on perceptions of the innovation, not perceptions of *using* the innovation.[14] We therefore find included in the expanded construct the phrase "use of the innovation," and this phrase should be transposed into the definition for relative advantage, compatibility, complexity, observability, and trialability.

Use of an innovation is the key to the innovation's diffusion but it is important to note that there is a distinction between attitudes toward an innovation and attitudes toward using an innovation. The importance of attitude is explained by the *Theory of Reasoned Action* and later by the *Theory of Planned Behavior.*[15] These theories were designed to predict and explain human behavior in specific contexts. The Theory of Planned Behavior (see figure 2.1) was developed when it was noted that its predecessor, the Theory of Reasoned Action, did not deal with behaviors over which people have incomplete volitional control. As we have already noted, the issue of volitional control can affect Internet diffusion in the workplace, where acceptance of Internet technology may be as much an artifact of these technologies being imposed as it is an indication of technology adoption by the workers themselves.

Figure 2.1. Theory of Planned Behavior

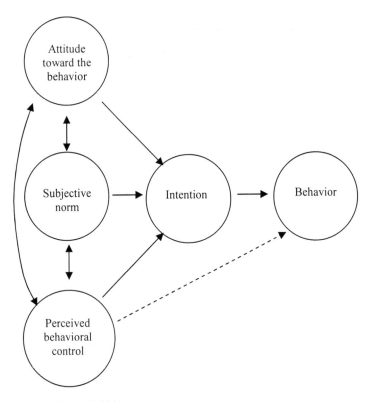

Source: Ajzen (1991)

The Theory of Planned Behavior focuses on the individual's intention to perform a given behavior or the motivational factors that influence the behavior. The general rule is that the stronger the intention to perform a particular action, the more likely it is that it *will* be performed by the individual. The caveat to this relationship is the extent to which a person can decide at will whether to perform this behavior or not. While some behaviors are prescribed by the choices that an individual can make, many behaviors depend on a range of nonmotivational factors within the overall context of use: resources, time, money, other people, and so on. These conditions describe or qualify the level of *actual control* that an individual has over his or her choice to exhibit a behavior or not. The level of actual control is of course important, but it is the concept of *perceived behavioral control*, that is, what the individual *thinks* about the level of control he or she has, that plays the more significant role in determining intentions and actions.

The Theory of Planned Behavior states that the performance of a behavior is a joint function of intentions and perceived behavioral control. The predictive validity of this theory depends on three factors:

1. The measures of intention and of perceived behavioral control must correspond to, or be compatible with, the behavior that is to be predicted.

In the context of our discussion of the Internet, this means that the intentions and perceptions of control must be assessed in relation to the behavior of interest and the specific context in which this behavior will occur. If the behavior to be predicted is use of the Internet to purchase a book, for example, then we must assess intentions to buy a book using the Internet—not simply intention to use the Internet or intention to buy a book.

2. Intentions and perceived behavioral control must remain stable between the time when they are assessed and the time the behavior is observed.

In this case, we need to be conscious of the impact that intervening events may have in terms of changing intentions or altering perceptions of behavioral control. If the original measures for these variables change, then accurate prediction of behavior is no longer possible.

3. The extent to which perceptions of behavioral control re-
    alistically reflect actual control.[16]

The relative importance of intentions and perceived behavioral control vary across situations and behaviors. The Theory of
Reasoned Action has been used to explain the influence of attitude on a range of behaviors, including the acceptance and use of
information technology. It underpins the Technology Acceptance
Model (TAM),[17] for example.

The Technology Acceptance Model (see figure 2.2) pos-
its that an individual's acceptance of information technology is
based on beliefs, attitudes, intentions, and behaviors. It pays particular attention to the affective response by individuals to technological innovation. The attitude that an individual has toward
technology use and adoption decisions is the key mediating construct, and an individual's attitude is determined by beliefs about
the perceived usefulness of the innovation. This is a subjective
judgment by the individual of the measure of utility offered by
the innovation. The second attitude relates to the individual's
perception of the ease of use of the innovation. The individual in
this case is estimating the amount of cognitive effort required to
adopt the technology or use it in a particular work context. Two
other features of the TAM draw on the relationship between use
and behavioral intention to use. In this case, attitude toward use
relates to an individual's perception of how desirable it will be to
use a particular innovation. Behavioral intention to use, on the
other hand, is a measure of the actual likelihood that a person
will use the innovation or technology.

Personal Innovativeness

With this background in mind, let us now return to our discussion of personal innovativeness. The significant recurring theme
that appears in theories of technology acceptance is that individual perceptions of the innovation or technology are critical.
These are the perceptions that the individual has about the

Figure 2.2. Technology Acceptance Model

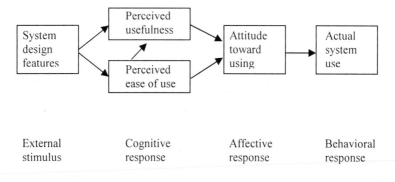

Source: Davis (1993)

characteristics of the technology or innovation, as well as the perceptions that the individual has concerning how the innovation might be used. It is important to accept both constructs but the next step toward our objective of a better understanding of technology acceptance by individuals is the valuing of individual differences. In particular, it has been argued that technology acceptance can depend on the individual difference variable of personal innovativeness.[18] Personal innovativeness is a predictor of how perceptions of a technology or innovation are formed and the role these might play in the formation of usage intentions.[19]

Personal innovativeness has been the focus for work exploring technological innovation for some time, but it has generally been used as an "ex post descriptor of behavior."[20] We need methods to explicate and measure this concept, and the first step toward achieving this goal is to see the distinction between global innovativeness and domain-specific innovativeness.[21] *Global innovativeness* is a characteristic that all individuals possess to some degree. It refers to a level of "willingness to change." In the context of the Internet, the general impact of this characteristic has been manifest in the levels of adoption of Internet technology by what we call the "general public." Global innovativeness has been criticized, however, as having low predictive power when applied to specific adoption decisions.[22]

Domain-specific innovativeness, by contrast, can be measured (like attitude and personality variables) and exerts a significant influence within a domain of activity, for example, a professional context. This is demonstrated by research into the innovation and application of Internet technologies in a wide range of professional settings. A detailed discussion of domain-specific innovativeness occurs in chapter 4 of this book, where research data are analyzed to reveal how members of various professional groups are using the Internet and its technologies.

The theoretical construction called *Personal Innovativeness for Information Technology Adoption* focuses on domain specific innovativeness.[23] This construct describes "a relatively stable descriptor of individuals that is invariant across situational considerations" within the domain of information technology. It is "the willingness of an individual to try out any new information technology."[24] Personal innovativeness influences both the causes and consequences of individual perceptions of technology. The characteristic behaviors of innovators in the domain of information technology are that these individuals tend to

- have greater mass-media exposure
- place less reliance on the subjective evaluation of information technologies by other members of their social system
- cope with higher levels of uncertainty and take risks
- require fewer positive perceptions of an information technology for adoption[25]

Conclusion

In conclusion, the diffusion of innovation through the beliefs, attitudes and actions of individuals and the interactions of people with other people (in contexts and across contexts) has been observed empirically and described theoretically. We have a rich set of frameworks that justify and explain our focus upon the attitudes and actions of people as the building blocks for understanding the phenomenon of the Internet.

There are just two more foundational pieces to the theoretical puzzle that we call the "user's view of the Internet." In the next chapter, we turn our attention to explaining the framework that is guiding practice in a number of the professional fields that have a keen interest in the way the Internet is shaping our lives. This framework applies some of the social psychology that has been at the heart of our discussion of technology acceptance and diffusion. It is called the user-oriented paradigm. Some of the professional fields that are informed by this perspective are business and education, technology fields such as computer science and engineering, and the spectrum of professions that serve the expanding information industry, including librarians, information managers, and information system designers. These professional fields are key stakeholders in the social formulations, individual and professional applications, and technological manifestations of the Internet. They are the practical and theoretical beneficiaries—also the shapers—of the user's view of the Internet.

The second foundational aspect that we need to address is finding and explaining the metatheoretical abstractions that justify our focus on Internet users. We need to explain why and how our focus on Internet use by people provides us with a deeper level understanding of the Internet phenomenon. We reach this objective at the end of chapter 3 and this sets the scene for the detailed synthesis of research data that appears in chapter 4.

Notes

1. Giovanni Dosi, "Sources, Procedures, and Microeconomic Effects of Innovation," *Journal of Economic Literature* 26, no. 3 (1988).

2. Stephen E. Arnold, *Publishing on the Internet: A New Medium for a New Millennium* (Calne, England: Infonortics, 1996).

3. Gary C. Moore and Izak Benbasat, "Development of an Instrument to Measure the Perceptions of Adopting an Information Technology Innovation," *Information Systems Research* 2, no. 3 (1991).

4. E.g., Shirley Taylor and Peter A. Todd, "Understanding Information Technology Usage: A Test of Competing Models," *Information Systems Research* 6, no. 2 (1995).

5. Ritu Agarwal and Jayesh Prasad, "A Conceptual and Operational Definition of Personal Innovativeness in the Domain of Information Technology," *Information Systems Research* 9, no. 2 (1998).

6. Everett M. Rogers, *Diffusion of Innovations*, 3d ed. (New York: Free Press, 1983).

7. Fareena Sultan and Lillian Chan, "The Adoption of New Technology: The Case of Object-Oriented Computing in Software Companies," *IEEE Transactions on Engineering Management* 47, no. 1 (2000).

8. Moore and Benbasat, "Development of an Instrument to Measure Perceptions," 195.

9. L. G. Tornatzky and K. J. Klein, "Innovation Characteristics and Innovation Adoption-Implementation: A Meta-Analysis of Findings," *IEEE Transactions on Engineering Management* EM-29, no. 1 (1982).

10. Moore and Benbasat, "Development of an Instrument to Measure Perceptions."

11. Moore and Benbasat, "Development of an Instrument to Measure Perceptions," 195.

12. Harry Bruce, *Internet, AARNet, and Academic Work: A Longitudinal Study* (Canberra, Australia: Australian Government Publication Service, 1996).

13. Bruce, *Internet, AARNet, and Academic Work*, 59.

14. Moore and Benbasat, "Development of an Instrument to Measure Perceptions."

15. Icek Ajzen and Martin Fishbein, *Understanding Attitudes and Predicting Social Behavior* (Englewood Cliffs, N.J.: Prentice-Hall, 1980); Icek Ajzen, "The Theory of Planned Behavior," *Organizational Behavior and Human Decision Processes* 50 (1991).

16. Ajzen, "The Theory of Planned Behavior," 185.

17. Fred D. Davis, "Perceived Usefulness, Perceived Ease of Use, and User Acceptance of Information Technology," *MIS Quarterly* 13, no. 3 (1989).

18. Agarwal and Prasad, "A Conceptual and Operational Definition of Personal Innovativeness"; Ritu Agarwal and Jayesh Prasad,

"Are Individual Differences Germane to the Acceptance of New Information Technologies?" *Decision Sciences* 30, no. 2 (1999).

19. Agarwal and Prasad, "A Conceptual and Operational Definition of Personal Innovativeness."

20. Agarwal and Prasad, "A Conceptual and Operational Definition of Personal Innovativeness," 206.

21. Agarwal and Prasad, "A Conceptual and Operational Definition of Personal Innovativeness."

22. Dorothy Leonard-Barton and Isabelle DesChamps, "Managerial Influence in the Implementation of New Technology," *Management Science* 34, no. 10 (1988).

23. Agarwal and Prasad, "A Conceptual and Operational Definition of Personal Innovativeness."

24. Agarwal and Prasad, "A Conceptual and Operational Definition of Personal Innovativeness," 206.

25. Agarwal and Prasad, "A Conceptual and Operational Definition of Personal Innovativeness."

Chapter 3

A Focus on Usings

In the past twenty-five years or so, we have seen what some have referred to as a user-centered revolution.[1] This revolution is manifest in the policy, theory, methodology, and practice of a range of disciplines and fields of study. The terminologies used to describe a focus on the beneficiaries or recipients of services, products, systems, or professional actions vary. Engineers design end-user technologies. Businesses, organizations, and institutions claim to be client centered, customer oriented, or market driven. The education field is learner centered.

Various stakeholders in the development of the Internet have developed versions of the user-centered revolution but overall we can see a shift from technology to people, from product to service, from outcome to process, and so on. The common ground is a focus on people—user oriented, people centered, user based, human centered, user responsive, and so on. The user focus is an amalgam of methods, approaches, and techniques that provide professions and disciplines with ways to define, understand, explain, measure, and ultimately serve the needs of people. This may involve the design and development of new practices, systems, services, resources, products, and technologies. Central to our focus on the Internet is that the user orientation means that the intuitions of designers and engineers and the levels and scale of technical innovation are no longer sufficient for prescribing technological development agendas.

Technological innovation is no longer being driven by the potential of technology or the research agendas of technicians and engineers but rather by the needs that people have for using these technologies in their daily professional and personal lives.

It is difficult to know how the contemporary focus on people (users, audiences) across various disciplines has been manifest in the evolution, development, and diffusion of the Internet. In recent years the Internet has become a broad-based information and communication infrastructure. We may wonder, could this have occurred in the absence of a focus on people by the stakeholders of Internet development? Equally, it is difficult to know just how much of the agenda for change and innovation has been specifically driven by those who espouse and practice a user orientation. Nevertheless, the Internet as it is defined today is not so much the internetworking of computers as it is the internetworking of people and services that address the needs of people. Chapter 1 of this book, which described and expounded the evolution and end-user provenance of the Internet, introduced us to the proposition that we can best understand the Internet by understanding the people who use it. In chapter 2 we introduced the theories that elaborate the role that people collectively and individually play in technology diffusion. What follows from this introduction is the proposition that we should view Internet development in terms of the ongoing or future needs and uses of people in various contexts.

Is this a reasonable proposition? The notion that operational effectiveness should override design efficiency as the driving force for innovation[2] would certainly have been novel (some might say impossible) in the early days of the ARPA experiments, for example. When computers were the size of large rooms and enormously expensive, it would have been difficult to imagine the needs of an individual user as the design imperative. The technology was primitive and inflexible. It could be claimed also that as the communities of users of the fledgling Internet evolved from the middle up, there was also a camaraderie of shared experience that created an elite user type that rejected the idea of making the Internet easy to use on the basis that "newbie" users should be required to undergo a rite of passage in the form of system learning that all dedicated users of the new infrastructure had undergone before them.[3]

In the early 1990s the huge increase in novice and unaffiliated Internet users, together with an increasingly flexible technology, swept aside these sentiments and constraints. Broader acceptance of the user-oriented perspective coincided with technology developing to a level where user-oriented ways of thinking and designing were feasible and practical. As Donald Norman states in his article entitled "Toward Human-Centered Design," by the mid-1990s, we found that we could "make machines that fit human needs, independent of mechanical constraints."[4]

Contemporary Internet technologies could, therefore, be more responsive to the demands of people wanting to use the network because our technical knowledge had increased, but broader acceptance of the user-oriented paradigm also depended on an increase in the numbers and types of Internet users.

Researchers must develop techniques for collecting data that facilitate deeper understandings of the characteristics of system or service users, but they must also be willing to accept the value of an accumulating volume of research into the behaviors and perceptions of system users. In late 1992, the author was astounded, for example, to find that the communication and computer engineers responsible for the development of the Australian Academic and Research Network had not studied the users of this network in any way prior to or during the development of this national infrastructure. While it might be argued that researchers had few users that they could study at this time (there were just a lot of nonusers and potential users of the network), there was, in fact, an abundance of research about people using electronic information environments that developers could have referred to. For example, at this time, researchers were able to characterize the users of developing networked systems as highly motivated by work outcomes, as opposed to design elegance or data structure. Research had also found that people wanted answers, not pointers; in other words, document delivery, not information retrieval. It was also known that users wanted to minimize the cognitive load of information-searching in an electronic environment and to maximize their enjoyment of the process.[5] Clearly, this research had arisen from, and been informed by, the user-oriented paradigm.

Research through the 1990s has continued to have a user-oriented focus and data from this work and what it tells us about the user's view of the Internet will be analyzed in detail in the next chapter of this book. Before doing so, it is important to note the broad acceptance of the user-oriented perspective across a range of disciplines and professional fields that have a significant interest in the development and use of the Internet. For this reason, I would like to turn to a description of how the focus on users and people has developed in the fields of business, education, cognitive engineering, and information science. This will lead us to a refinement of the user-oriented paradigm based on science studies and information science. The result is an analytical lens for teasing through data collected by Internet researchers (described in chapter 4) and converting this data to theoretical constructions that are the users' view of the Internet (chapter 5).

Client-Centered Marketing and Participatory Management

In the world of business, organizations and institutions (both private and public) are accommodating new ways of thinking about management and marketing. This new paradigm has been variously referred to as person-centered or participatory management and customer-centered, market-driven, or client-centered marketing. The genesis of this paradigm is difficult to determine. Certainly, it has a theoretical foundation, but in the hard-nosed, practical world of business, new marketing and leadership principles can also emerge from successful or exemplary cases that demonstrate new techniques for growing market share, business growth, or effective management. Technology and innovation are also key factors. A growing focus on customers and individual clients can be traced to the pressure placed on businesses by savvy consumers. Customers know that technology and innovation make customization and individual attention to their needs possible. This new dynamic in the market has prompted a shift for many organizations away from product-centered operations toward more service-centered business practice.

Traditionally, marketing has been based on a simple transaction paradigm. The principles of this paradigm are product, price, place, and promotion. A company develops and produces a product, identifies customers for the product, and then identifies techniques for convincing customers to buy the product. The company makes customers aware of the product through mass marketing based on advertising and promotion. The customers are told what to buy, and the marketing strategies are based on promoting the company's image and credibility. With transaction marketing, the focus is on achieving sales of the product by selling the products' features. To some extent, customer service is an afterthought. The business that operates under this paradigm has a limited commitment to the customer. The business makes contact with the customer only at the point of sale, and quality is primarily the concern of the production unit, not the sales and marketing department.

In contrast to the transaction paradigm, customer-focused marketing is based on developing a relationship with the individuals that the organization serves. This may appear impossible or, at best—from a mass-market perspective—far from cost-effective. It is, however, possible, with the use of interactive databases, for a business to target its customers one at a time and to set the goal of satisfying the individual needs of each customer in terms of how these individuals define their own requirements. Collecting information from customers is obviously of great importance to this paradigm. This is sometimes referred to as developing a learning relationship with the customers, and the information gathered is critical to the business that operates under this paradigm because the customer or client is not seen simply as a series of transactions but rather as a component of the business—a member of the production team, a critical factor in driving the business forward. The business is, in this way, market driven as opposed to marketing driven. Table 3.1, taken from Kathleen Allen's 1999 work *Growing and Managing an Entrepreneurial Business,*[6] helps to distinguish the new marketing paradigm from traditional marketing strategy.

Table 3.1. The Changing Marketing Paradigm

The Traditional Marketing Strategy	The New Approach to Marketing for the Twenty-First Century
Market driven	Marketing driven
Producer capacity orientation	Customer demand orientation
Market share focus	Market creation focus
Mass marketing techniques	One-to-one relationship marketing
Focus on increasing customers to increase sales volume	Focus on seeking and retaining customers as stakeholders

Source: K. Allen (1999), 270.

Business leadership and management are undergoing a similar shift in emphasis. This shift emerged from efforts related to quality improvement models for business and was first described as participatory management and later person-centered leadership.[7]

Participatory management is a management strategy that has captured the imagination of large and small companies. Its origins can be traced to the employee involvement movement that took off in Japan and parts of Europe and the United States between 1920 and 1950.[8] During the 1980s, employee involvement was recognized as an important part of a comprehensive management model called Total Quality Management (TQM). TQM involves process improvement, customer relations, statistical graphing, problem solving, brainstorming, the establishment of priorities, information sharing, and departmental communication.[9] A number of companies across the United States focused on participatory management as the key component of TQM with some notable successes. The general thrust of participatory management is to create a corporate culture or institutional environment where individual excellence can flourish.[10]

Among the success stories associated with participatory management, there have also been some notable failures, however, and this has led to the development of *person-centered leadership*. Person-centered leadership acknowledges the importance of empowering workers, but also repositions the worker as an individual at the center of company attention:

> Management is concerned with recognizing and supporting personal and family needs, developing personal well-being, and listening carefully to individual complaints. Management proceeds person by person.[11]

The essential feature of this new leadership model is to involve those who are doing the work in the decision-making process—to use the expertise of the worker. Often this requires creative team construction and management. It also relies on a commitment to life-long learning by the worker. Learning must be at the center of the corporate culture.

In short, there has been a paradigm shift in management and corporate leadership—away from mechanistic, bureaucratic, top-down organizational structures. The new management model is flatter, inclusive, and participative. Leadership acknowledges the importance of the individual worker to productivity and quality improvement in corporate and organizational culture.

Learner-Centered Education

The culture of the individual has also permeated the educational sector. While businesses have been acknowledging the importance to corporate progress of the life-long learning of workers, the educational sector has been considering new models for understanding and facilitating educational processes. The trend here is referred to as *learner-centered education* and, like the other paradigm shifts discussed in this chapter, features of this new perspective can be contrasted with a preexisting or traditional viewpoint—in this case, teacher-centered learning.

With teacher-centered learning, the teacher is responsible for and makes all decisions related to the learning environment. The teacher decides what is to be learned, how this content is to be learned, and how student learning will be assessed. The curriculum is often set in predetermined, mandated packages that individual teachers are expected to follow. There are choices that the teacher can make about delivery, interpretation of content, resources, and timetabling, and these decisions will be made according to their preferred teaching style, expertise, and experiences. In teacher-centered learning, the learner is less responsible for what they learn and less active in the learning process. Learning is linear and the educational environment has set patterns and routines.

Teacher-centered learning is a commonly applied model, so most readers will be familiar with its advantages and disadvantages from personal experience. These have been summarized as follows:

Advantages
- The teacher can be certain that the students are exposed to all the knowledge and concepts the teacher feels are appropriate for the targeted curricular unit.
- This method is universally recognized by students, teachers, parents, and administrators.

Disadvantages

- Not all students are homogeneous in background, knowledge, and experience; nor are they homogeneous in learning abilities in different areas or in their pace and style of learning.
- The students are generally passive recipients and do not "learn to learn."
- Teachers usually cannot guarantee that students' experiences will be useful once they leave the class.[12]

The disadvantages of teacher-centered learning draw attention to the characteristics of an alternative approach to teaching and learning: student-centered learning. Here again, the primacy of the individual is reinforced. With student-centered learning, each learner is seen as an individual with a particular background, set of experiences, beliefs, educational needs, skills and abilities, and learning style preferences. The teacher facilitates learning through investigation, discovery, and problem solving, but it is the student who is seen as responsible for his or her own learning. Some refer to this framework as *authentic learning* because the student determines what he or she needs to master while grappling with real-world problems. There is a strong emphasis on matching learning events to the individual skills, aptitudes, and interests of the individual learner. The learner and the teacher are positioned as collaborators in the learning enterprise. Students learn how to learn, and life-long learning is the ultimate goal.

Focus on the learner is the key. In 1990, the American Psychological Association (APA) and the Mid-continent Regional Educational Laboratory (McREL) created a task force on psychology in education that resulted in the publication of fourteen learner-centered principles (see table 3.2). The full text of these principles can be found online at the APA website.[13]

Table 3.2. Learner-Centered Psychological Principles

	Cognitive and Metacognitive Factors
1	*Nature of the learning process.* The learning of complex subject matter is most effective when it is an intentional process of constructing meaning from information and experience.
2	*Goals of the learning process.* The successful learner, over time and with support and instructional guidance, can create meaningful, coherent representations of knowledge.
3	*Construction of knowledge.* The successful learner can link new information with existing knowledge in meaningful ways.
4	*Strategic thinking.* The successful learner can create and use a repertoire of thinking and reasoning strategies to achieve complex learning goals.
5	*Thinking about thinking.* Higher-order strategies for selecting and monitoring mental operations facilitate creative and critical thinking.
6	*Context of learning.* Learning is influenced by environmental factors, including culture, technology, and instructional practices.
	Motivational and Affective Factors
7	*Motivational and emotional influences on learning.* What and how much is learned is influenced by the learner's motivation. Motivation to learn, in turn is influences by the individual's emotional states.
8	*Intrinsic motivation to learn.* The learner's creativity, higher-order thinking, and natural curiosity all contribute to motivation to learn. Intrinsic motivation is stimulated by tasks of optimal novelty and difficulty, relevant to personal interests, and providing for personal choice and control.
9	*Effects of motivation on effort.* Acquisition of complex knowledge and skills requires extended learner effort and guided practice. Without the learner's motivation to learn, the willingness to exert this effort is unlikely without coercion.

Table 3.2. Learner-Centered Psychological Principles *(continued)*

	Development and Social Factors
10	*Developmental influences on learning.* As individuals develop, there are different opportunities and constraints for learning. Learning is most effective when differential development within and across physical, intellectual, emotional, and social domains is taken into account.
11	*Social influences on learning.* Learning is influenced by social interactions, interpersonal relations, and communication with others.
	Individual differences
12	*Individual differences in learning.* Learners have different strategies, approaches, and capabilities for learning that are a function of prior experiences and heredity.
13	*Learning and diversity.* Learning is most effective when differences in learners' linguistic, cultural, and social backgrounds are taken into account.
14	*Standards and assessment.* Setting appropriately high and challenging standards and assessing the learner as well as learning progress—including diagnostic, process, and outcome assessment—are integral parts of the learning process.

Source: Bonk and Cunningham (1998), 29.

The advantages and disadvantages of student-centered learning are as follows:

Advantages
- Students do "learn to learn" so that they can meet the life-long need to adapt to contemporary knowledge, challenges, and problems they will need to encounter in the future.

- Students acquire the ability to evaluate their own strengths and weaknesses, to determine their own needs, and to learn to meet those needs.

Disadvantages

- Student-centered learning creates many organizational problems. To those not familiar with this type of curriculum, it looks messy and somewhat hard to manage.
- The student-centered approach can create insecurity in students, parents and faculty.[14]

In summary, the disadvantages of student-centered learning focus primarily on the management challenges of the approach rather than on the effectiveness of the approach in terms of enhancing student learning.

This has not swayed proponents of the approach, who see recent developments in technology and in particular, the World Wide Web, as a fertile context for an educational approach that will challenge the learner to make sense of new information by linking new information with old or the known with the unknown and to think creatively.[15] Indeed, the student-centered approach emphasizes the social plane of the individual as the origin of mental activity and growth.[16] The focus is on the individual within a learning community and the World Wide Web is regarded as a learning environment that has enormous potential to extend the scale, scope, and range of involvement and collaboration for the individual and endorsement of student-centered learning. Indeed, the World Wide Web provides many of the tools and structures that can support student-centered learning. It offers an opportunity to blend technological advances with contemporary pedagogical thinking to create what some refer to as "learner centered technology."[17] Technology-rich learning environments are a fertile context for reevaluating the role of the teacher and the processes of learning. The expense of technology infrastructure does warrant theoretical or research underpinning rather than relying on assumptions that the learner will benefit.

The World Wide Web is also a fertile ground for adult education. The concept of life-long learning is closely tied to the learner-centered perspective. In adult education, learner-centered approaches have been developed by theorists and writers like Malcolm Knowles,[18] who believed that adult learning should be based on the individual learner's interests, abilities, needs, and goals. Knowles's approach relies on the teacher developing an empathy with the adult learner. He called the system that he developed *andragogy,* "the art and science of helping adults learn."[19]

In summary, the paradigm that underpins educational processes and practices in the contemporary school, higher education, and adult learning environments is centered on learners and learning communities. Emerging technologies and pedagogies are therefore being analyzed and evaluated from this perspective.

User-Centered Design and Cognitive Engineering

Consistent with the theme of the culture of the individual and the user-centered revolution is the perception that there may be a mismatch between progress in the human domain and technological or industrial advancement. Some have expressed the concern that we may experience problems with a "culture lag" the more we fail to understand the true nature of the human adaptation to industry and innovation. It has been argued that the critical questions of this mismatch or lag in knowledge need to be answered by the social rather than the physical sciences so that we can begin to predict and control the benefits of innovation and development.[20]

Manifestations of these concerns began to appear in the work of sociological technical systems professionals who, from the 1950s, were examining the technical and social structure of work systems and identifying, for example, that various cultures have differing sociotechnical traditions. Concern for the individual has also found expression in the development of what have been called "human-centered" and "work-oriented" man-machine systems and the emergence of the human factors professions concerned with applying our scientific knowledge of humans to the design of man-machine interface systems. Human factors professionals apply knowledge from cognitive science, psychology, systems theory, sociology, and organizational theory to the central consideration of the human in technology design and implementation.

The background to what is now known as "user-centered design"[21] can be traced back to the mid-1980s when Norman and Draper suggested that systems should be designed to account for the goals that people are trying to achieve when they use any type of system.[22] Norman actually coined the term *cognitive engineering* to describe this form of design, which he wanted to distinguish from cognitive psychology and human factors—a combination of psychology and computer science.[23] The main aim in cognitive engineering for Norman was the application of what we know about human thoughts and actions to the design and construction of machines.

User-centered design is based fundamentally on knowing what people need to do with the machine or tool being designed. This requires an understanding of the elements of the tasks to be performed and the values that may be inherent in this task. It also requires an understanding of how individuals make a translation from the psychological elements of task execution and completion with the physical tools or systems that will enable satisfactory solutions. There are two major goals:

1. To understand the fundamental principles behind human action and performance that are relevant for the development of engineering principles of design
2. To devise systems that are pleasant to use—the goal is neither efficiency nor ease nor power, although these are all to be desired, but rather systems that are pleasant, even fun: to produce . . . pleasurable engagement[24]

The goals of a person are expressed in terms that are relevant to that individual. For user-centered design or cognitive engineering, these are psychological variables. On the other hand, the mechanisms of the system are expressed in terms relative to it, and these are considered the variables that constrain or define the physical parameters of design. This split between the psychological and the physical provides the construct for developing a theory of action that can guide design. The Theory of Action proposed by Norman defines the design process as bridging the gap between the goals of people and the physical system. [25] This gap can be bridged by starting from either the system side or the user side. The designer can start from the system side and bridge the gap (in this direction referred to as the *gulf of evaluation*) by designing the interface to the system in such a way that it makes a best match with the psychological needs of the user. The designer needs to know about the user's intentions relevant to the system and the sequence of actions that the user must follow in order to achieve the task. In the other direction (referred to as the *gulf of execution*), the gap is bridged by the user's perception of the system's capacity to serve his or her goals and intentions. This is achieved when the designer builds effective output characteristics for the system interface.

The Theory of Action identifies seven stages of user activity which help to align user goals with physical systems: establishing the goal, forming the intention, specifying the action sequence, executing the action, perceiving the system state, interpreting the state, and evaluating the system state with respect to the goals and intentions.

The steps to user-centered design resolve fundamentally through stages in a process aimed at achieving knowledge of the characteristics of the users of a design artifact and then reflecting these characteristics and perceptions into the prototyping, developing, and testing of the design. Bryce Allen provides some background to what these elements of user modeling ought to be by reviewing the models[26] of Dillon,[27] Olson and Olson,[28] and Mahling.[29]

The Dillon model for user-centered design has five steps:

1. Stakeholder identification
2. User analysis
3. Task analysis
4. Specification, and
5. Prototype[30]

The Olson and Olson approach to user-centered design is designated by a set of ten questions:

1. Analyze the goal: what is the purpose of the activity?
2. How should the activity be done, ideally?
3. What potential problems are there with doing it the way it is typically done?
4. How do current technologies or processes support this activity?
5. What are the limits to these?
6. What are the requirements for new aids?
7. How can information technology meet these requirements?
8. What costs may be incurred by new technology aids?
9. What special characteristics of the specific domain must be taken into account?
10. What are the potential differences from groups with various natures and size?[31]

The Mahling model has six steps:

1. Goal analysis,
2. Domain/task analysis,
3. User/group analysis,
4. Model formation,
5. System design and implementation, and
6. Usability testing[32]

Information Science and the User-Oriented Paradigm

The three models for user-centered design in the previous section come from cognitive engineering and computing. Allen, on the other hand, is an information scientist so he is primarily interested in the design of information systems. His model for user-centered design has five steps:

1. Needs analysis
2. Task analysis
3. Resource analysis
4. User modeling
5. Design for usability

To understand the provenance of user-centered design in information science, it is necessary to examine the user-oriented paradigm. The user-oriented paradigm is, to some extent, an amalgam of sociological, psychological,[33] and cognitive[34] viewpoints that focus attention on the information user. The first explicit use of the term *user-oriented* (for information science) appeared in a chapter of the *Annual Review of Information Science and Technology* (ARIST) in 1986. The authors of this chapter (Brenda Dervin and Michael Nilan) were commissioned to review the literature on information needs and uses between 1978 and 1986. The result was a seminal work that coined the term *user-oriented paradigm* and explicated the various assumptions that underpin the work of information researchers and practitioners who focus on users rather than systems. From this point on, information scientists had a framework for describing a particular perspective for their work in developing systems and services that would meet the needs of information users. User perspectives enriched the discipline. Researchers described themselves as user centered or user centric. Others focused on the problem space of the user[35] or the user's cognitive discontinuities[36] or uncertainties[37] that prompt people to interact with information systems and environments. The perceptions of individual users of information became the centerpiece consideration for information service and system design.

As a conceptual framework, the user-oriented paradigm is an alternative to the physical[38] or system-oriented paradigm.[39] The system-oriented paradigm was the dominant approach to research in the discipline of information science up until the late 1970s. The origins of the system-oriented paradigm are generally traced back to 1953, when tests in Britain and the United States were conducted to evaluate the performance of alternative approaches to subject indexing and retrieval. These so-called Cranfield tests marked a watershed in the discipline of information science.[40] As a conceptual framework for the discipline, the system-oriented paradigm which emerged is characterized by assumptions about key concepts like information, information need, information seeking, information users, and information use. Research that is underpinned by the system-oriented paradigm generally focuses on the extent to which an information system has been used and reports on any barriers that may prevent, or diminish satisfaction with, use of the system.

When Dervin and Nilan articulated their views on the development of the user-oriented paradigm in information science, they described the user-oriented paradigm by contrasting its assumptions with those of the physical or system-oriented paradigm.[41] They achieved this by comparing the paradigms under the categories of assumptions, which appear in table 3.3. Dervin and Nilan summed up their perception of the user-oriented paradigm by noting:

> It focuses on the user . . . examines the system only as seen by the user. . . . [It] asks many how questions . . . [like] how do people define needs in different situations, how do they present these needs to systems, and how do they make use of what the system offers them.[42]

Table 3.3. System-Oriented and User-Oriented Assumptions

System-Oriented Paradigm	User-Oriented Paradigm
Objective Information Information has constant meaning. It is a commodity or thing. It can be transported. It reflects an absolute correspondence with reality. It will convey the same meaning to all users.	*Subjective Information* Information does not transmit constant meaning. Information users interpret information and create sense or meaning in accordance with their unique model or image of the world
Mechanistic Passive Users Users are regarded as information processing systems. Being informed or benefiting from information is assumed to result directly from document delivery with no intervening user behavior.	*Constructivist Active Users* The user constructs need out of situations and is actively involved in information transfer. The user undertakes activities that will induce sensemaking. The user is actively involved from the time the information arises to the point of problem resolution.
Transituationality Users with similar characteristics in similar situations will react in similar ways, use information similarly, and make similar decisions. The information behavior of users is described in ways that apply across situations.	*Situationality* An individual's responsiveness to information is governed by a range of variables that are unique to the individual and to the information problem that the user is engaging. Individuals operate from different centers at different times.

Table 3.3. System-Oriented and User-Oriented Assumptions *(continued)*

System-Oriented Paradigm	User-Oriented Paradigm
Atomistic View of Experience The focus is on user behavior at the point of intersection with the information system; the moment of contact and exchange.	*Holistic View of Experience* A user's behavior is studied in terms of those factors that lead to an encounter with an information system and the consequences of such an encounter. A broader view of information behavior from the time need arises until it no longer exists.
External Behavior Very concrete. Contact with a system is the basic indicator of information need. Focus on what can be observed as overt behavior.	*Internal Cognitions* Acknowledges the premise that what is going on inside a person's mind (the individual's model of the world) will shape the way information is interpreted and used. Interested in what people think as well as what they do when they engage in information behavior.
Chaotic Individuality Focus on individual information behavior will cause too much variation. Systems cannot accommodate individual interpretation. Individuality means chaos and prevents systematic research.	*Systematic Individuality* The complexity of individuality can be addressed in a way that is consistent with scientific investigation.

Source: Bruce and Todd (1993), 88-89.

The user-oriented paradigm, with its assumptions about information, information seeking, information need, and information users, has since been widely adopted by researchers in the information field. It has provided a framework for research examining information need,[43] information seeking,[44] system design,[45] a client focus in consumer research,[46] and the way users determine the relevance of the documents they retrieve.[47] In fact, by the beginning of the 1990s the user-oriented paradigm was regarded as a mainstream theoretical framework[48] that had already begun to spawn a number of related, user-based paradigms or perspectives that shaped research in information behavior during the ensuing decade.

One example is the cognitive viewpoint. Not all information researchers share precisely the same definition of the cognitive viewpoint, but there is a "kernel" of meaning which is common to most.[49] The essence of the viewpoint, and its importance to information research, is that it

> explicitly considers that the states of knowledge, beliefs and so on of human beings (or information processing devices) mediate (or interact with) that which they receive/ perceive or produce.[50]

The cognitive viewpoint is defined as an approach and set of constructs for understanding information behavior, which focuses fundamentally upon attributes of the individual. This view of information behavior endorses research that examines the cognitive and emotional motivations for information behavior that carry across contexts or are independent of context. The cognitive viewpoint does not study the context of information behavior and is, in this way, distinguished from the social cognitive view (discussed later) where context (particularly attributes of the social context) is the focus for explaining variations in human information behavior.

At the heart of the cognitive viewpoint rests the concept of *knowledge structures*. This concept has been borrowed from the cognitive sciences. Knowledge structures are the sets of concept relationships that comprise each individual's model of the world.

It is this model of the world that is seen to mediate an individual's information behavior. Each person will apply the knowledge structures that are required to perceive, interpret, modify, or transfer information. Information behavior research from the cognitive viewpoint acknowledges the thesis that

> any processing of information—whether perceptual (such as perceiving an object) or symbolic (such as understanding a sentence)—is mediated by a system of categories or concepts, which for the information processor, constitutes a representation or a model of his world.[51]

Information research that applies the cognitive viewpoint is therefore interested in studying how an individual will apply his or her model or view of the world to the processes of needing, seeking, giving, and using information.

By the start of the 1990s there had been numerous examples of information research that had focused on the user as an individual, cognitive being. The theoretical framework called the cognitive viewpoint and the focus on the individual as a unique information user had become well accepted and widely applied, leading Belkin to state that there was strong evidence to support the claim that "taking the cognitive viewpoint of information science can lead to highly beneficial results, in a variety of areas." Belkin further speculated:

> The cognitive viewpoint might serve as a means for integrating and relating work in a variety of areas of information science to one another, and therefore provide the structure for a unified and effective information science.[52]

To some extent Belkin's words proved to be prophetic for information research during the 1990s. Over this period, the work of information researchers identified with the cognitive approach focused on explaining variations in information behavior according to characteristics or attributes of the individual. A number of researchers attempted to generalize from observations of individuals or groups of individuals (researchers, students, scholars, library users).[53] These attempts have resulted in models of the information-seeking process that are context independent. Where the environment or situation is mentioned,[54] the term categorizes aspects or attributes of the individual's *self* rather than the social, professional, or information-seeking setting. This body of research reveals that there is an individual readiness to engage in information-seeking behavior that depends on various preconditions associated with a person's level of information arousal. It describes and analyzes a range of cognitive conditions and emotional responses that arise when people engage in information behavior. It also confirms that information-seeking behavior is a process or set of processes or stages that an individual moves through in space and time and that there are reliable methods for mapping these processes and observing the variations and consistent patterns of behavior that emerge.

This is not to say that information research has ignored context. Another category of contemporary research in this area, referred to collectively as *multifaceted approaches,*[55] gives a strong emphasis to context in explaining variations in information behavior. This body of work generally attempts to make a distinction between the context of work and the context of everyday life. In fact, many of these studies are focused on examining the information behaviors of professional people as they engage in their work in their work environment. There have been numerous studies of the information behavior of professionals such as engineers,[56] teachers,[57] health workers,[58] and academics.[59] A small number of studies have also recently emerged that focus on everyday information behaviors. Savolainen, for example, conducted a series of interviews with working-class and middle-class people in Finland to compare their information-seeking behavior.[60] This study elaborated distinctions between what the researcher called *way of life* and *mastery of life* in terms of information behavior. Way of life is the order that is created when people make choices in everyday life based on their individual preferences. Mastery of life is whether people actually adhere to their own preferences when they take on everyday activities. Savolainen found that people usually develop information-seeking habits as part of their mastery of life and that both way of life and mastery of life are affected by social, cultural, economic, and psychological factors.

Savolainen's work was informed by the *sensemaking* approach initiated by Dervin in the early 1970s. This approach has been widely used and constantly updated and developed as a metatheory for informing and guiding studies of information seeking through the 1980s and 1990s. Sensemaking addresses all types of contexts that can affect the information behaviors of people. Researchers in various areas such as media studies, education, health, and information science have used the approach, with several themes emerging:

- Humans are anchored in material conditions and at the same time have mind and spirit and can make abstractions, dream, feel, plan, have ambitions and fantasies, and tell stories.
- Humans are involved in a constant journey in time and space of sensemaking and sense-unmaking.
- Humans and their worlds are constantly evolving and their description therefore requires verbing.
- Human movement is impacted by forces, and those should be always considered.
- Ordinary human beings are theory makers.
- Humans can articulate emotions, spiritual experiences, and embodied unconscious.
- Patterns and connectivities among human beings take many forms, including the causal, spontaneous, and collaborative.
- No a priori assumption about human patterning should be made.
- The researcher should be self-conscious and self-reflexive.[61]

The most recent refinement of the user-oriented paradigm, called *social constructionism* or the *discourse analytic theory,* has an epistemological and ontological link to sensemaking.[62] In direct contrast to the cognitive viewpoint, social constructionism does not focus upon the mental representations and knowledge structures of the individual as the source of meanings, values, and ethical principles. Social constructionism views language as the primary shaper of observations and interpretations of the world. Information holds variable versions of reality that emerge from social interaction,[63] so knowledge and knowledge structures are not seen as subjective or unique to the individual. Rather, knowledge structures are produced by a shared system of meanings and are thus intersubjective.[64]

Social constructionism draws attention to flaws in the way variations in information behavior have been traditionally explained. Accepting that people create, search for, and use information in different ways, information scientists have generally explained these differences in terms of cognitive skills, knowledge states, motivations, educational levels, socioeconomic variations, problem situations, and so on. The problem is that individuals can have diverse social roles, tasks, and identities and it is impossible to get data on an individual's cognitive skills that aren't in some way contaminated by the cultural bias of the instrument used.

From the social constructionism viewpoint, the central problem that we face when we try to study information users and information using is the variability of knowledge formations. The production and use of information is connected to the variable social life-worlds and interests of people. This means that when we develop information systems, our central concern is not that people are incapable of conceptualizing their information needs or formulate need in ways that are different to information producers or information systems. The central problem is how can we develop systems that are able to incorporate the multiple viewpoints of people who will use them.[65]

Circulating Reference and Usings

In many professional and academic contexts, then, practitioners are thinking about people. The discourse, research, and practice of these fields is oriented toward users, has a user focus, or values world viewings from a user perspective. This theoretical framework sets the scene for the next stage of our journey toward the user's view of the Internet. Before embarking on this journey, however, we need to take one more theoretical step which will involve positioning the metatheoretic assumptions of the user-oriented paradigm through a blending of the work of Bruno Latour[66] with work by Brenda Dervin.[67] From this blending, we achieve the scientific and theoretical explanation for our focus on users and usings of the Internet. The concept of *usings* is Dervin's construct. I would like to return to usings after first introducing and explaining Latour's view of how science bridges the gap between mind and object through a process he defines as *circulating reference.*

Latour, who characterizes himself as a practitioner of the discipline called "science studies" (which pays particular attention to the details of scientific practice) describes *scientific practice* as a chain of transformations that allows us to bridge the gap between mind and object. The gap between mind and object is too broad, so in scientific efforts to understand the object, we characteristically engage in a succession of finely grained transformations that construct and transfer truth about the object. The transfer of truth about the object (the translation from matter to form) depends on the ability of each "link" in this chain of microtranslations to provide that bridge between mind and object. As Latour states, "Truth-value circulates here like electricity through a wire, so long as the circuit is not interrupted."[68]

Latour illustrated this chain of transformations in a description of a scientific expedition to the Amazon Forest (Boa Vista). In detail, he deconstructs the steps that a team of scientists takes when translating the object (the Boa Vista forest savanna) into a scientific report. He presents these microlevel moments of scientific translation as a chain of elements of representation (see figure 3.1).

Figure 3.1. Conceptions of Reference

Elements of representation

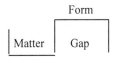

Chain of elements

Upstream

Representation

∞ ? ? ? ? ? ∞

Downstream

Source: Latour (1999)

Latour then elaborated the character of this translation by explaining that, as we move from the middle of the chain to its extremities, we are both losing something and gaining something. We are, through each information-producing scientific translation, losing the locality, particularity, materiality, multiplicity, and continuity of the object of study. Latour refers to this as *reduction*. At the same time, we are also gaining compatibility, standardization, text, calculation, circulation, and relative universality, which Latour calls *amplification* (see figure 3.2).

This construct contradicts a philosophical tradition that positions phenomena at the meeting point between objects and human understandings (what is in the human mind). Instead, as an alternative, Latour proposes that phenomena appear at each step of the phenomena are lost through reduction and others are gained through amplification (see figure 3.3). This chain of transformations starts at the middle and works outward toward extremities that are continually being pushed away (see figure 3.4).

Figure 3.2. Reduction and Amplification

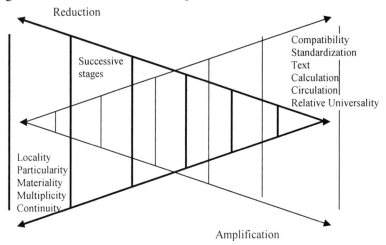

Source: Latour (1999)

Figure 3.3. Viewings of Phenomenon

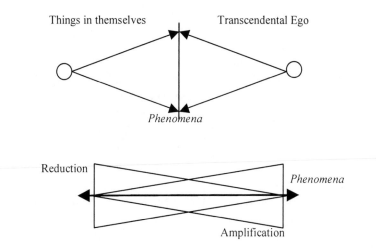

Source: Latour (1999)

Figure 3.4. Circulating Reference

Circulating reference

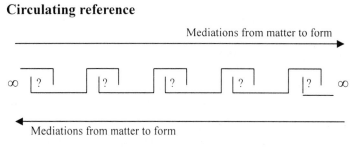

Source: Latour (1999)

With this construction in place, let us now turn our attention to some propositions recently offered by Dervin.[69] At the time, Dervin was responding to a background paper that was designed to facilitate preliminary discussion of information needs and information seeking for a digital libraries workshop. In her response, she draws attention to the metatheoretic assumptions that are the basis for our thinking about information needs and information seeking. Like Latour, she attempts to focus attention on the particular way that we look at the world. In terms of information needs and seeking, Dervin states, our attention is primarily turned to what we consider, as scientists, three discrete and discernible points of interest: contexts, users, and systems. Have we ever considered that users may not see or give any attention to these three points? From a users' point of view, do they exist, or is it the connection between these points (the behavings) that are of real interest—the micromoments of human use? Dervin calls these micromoments of real interest and significance *usings*. Users are not "real." What is "real" is usings and the world viewings, seekings, and valuings that they comprise.

The challenge is, then, how do we theorize users, contexts, systems, and usings? The answer proposed here is to see usings as the key elements of representation in Latour's conception of circulating reference. Where we are concerned with the object (Internet), our representation of this object is achieved through a chain of transformations made up of the micromoments of human usings of the Internet. The Internet as a composite of usings. As we constantly observe and represent (through insights from our researching) the Internet from its smallest constituent part (a using), stage by stage we reduce the complex phenomenon of the Internet (in Latour's case, this was the Boa Vista in the Amazon) so that we hold (understand) through this chain of elements of representation the essence and the explanation of the object study.

The goal for the rest of this book, then, is to examine and describe in detail the researching of Internet usings. In most cases, the research that will be analyzed was originally designed to focus on contexts, users, and systems, but the data have a richness that we can exploit for our purposes if we adjust the lens of our analysis to tease out a characterization of the micro-moments of Internet usings. We will see the phenomena of Internet circulating through these usings. This analysis will render representations that expose the user's view of the Internet.

Notes

1. Diane Nahl, "The User-Centered Revolution, 1970-1995," in *Encyclopedia of Library and Information Science*, ed. Allen Kent (New York: Marcel Dekker, 1998).

2. Nahl, "The User-Centered Revolution."

3. Donald A. Norman, *Turn Signals Are the Facial Expressions of Automobiles* (Reading, Mass.: Addison-Wesley, 1992).

4. Donald A. Norman, "Toward Human-Centered Design," *Technology Review* 96 (1993), 52.

5. Gary Marchionini, "Interfaces for End-User Information Seeking," *Journal of the American Society for Information Science* 43, no. 2 (1992).

6. Kathleen R. Allen, *Growing and Managing an Entrepreneurial Business* (Boston: Houghton Mifflin, 1999), 270.

7. Jeanne M. Plas, *Person-Centered Leadership: An American Approach to Participatory Management* (Thousand Oaks, Calif.: Sage, 1996).

8. Plas, *Person-Centered Leadership.*

9. Bill Creech, *The Five Pillars of TQM: How to Make Total Quality Management Work for You* (New York: Truman Talley Books/Dutton, 1994).

10. Lynne J. McFarland, Larry E. Senn, and John Childress, *Twenty-First-Century Leadership* (Los Angeles: Leadership Press, 1994).

11. Plas, *Person-Centered Leadership*, 60.

12. Neal A. Glasgow, *New Curriculum for New Times: A Guide to Student-Centered, Problem-Based Learning* (Thousand Oaks, Calif.: Corwin Press, 1997), 32-33.

13. American Psychological Association, Work Group of the American Psychological Association's Board of Educational Affairs,

"Learner-Centered Psychological Principles: A Framework for School Redesign and Reform," http://www.apa.org/ed/lcp.html, 1997 [accessed 5 July 2001].

14. Glasgow, *New Curriculum for New Times,* 35-36.

15. Curtis Jay Bonk and Thomas H. Reynolds, "Learner-Centered Web Instruction for Higher-Order Thinking, Teamwork, and Apprenticeship," in *Web-Based Instruction,* ed. Badrul Huda Khan (Englewood Cliffs, N.J.: Educational Technology Publications, 1997).

16. Ann L. Brown and Annemarie S. Palincsar, "Guided, Cooperative Learning and Individual Knowledge Acquisition," in *Cognition and Instruction: Issues and Agendas,* ed. L. Resnick (Hillsdale, N.J.: Lawrence Erlbaum Associates, 1989); G. M. Chang-Wells and G. Wells, "Dynamics of Discourse: Literacy and the Construction of Knowledge," in *Contexts for Learning: Sociocultural Dynamics in Children's Development,* ed. Ellice A. Forman, Norris Minick, and C. Addison Stone (New York: Oxford University Press, 1993); G. Salomon, "AI in Reverse: Computer Tools That Turn Cognitive," *Journal of Educational Computing Research* 4, no. 2 (1988).

17. Curtis Jay Bonk and Donald J. Cunningham, "Searching for Learner-Centered, Constructivist, and Sociocultural Components of Collaborative Educational Learning Tools," in *Electronic Collaborators: Learner-Centered Technologies for Literacy, Apprenticeship, and Discourse,* ed. Curtis Jay Bonk and Kira S. King (Mahwah, N.J.: Erlbaum Associates, 1998), 30.

18. Malcolm Shepard Knowles, *The Modern Practice of Adult Education: From Pedagogy to Andragogy* (New York: Cambridge Books, 1980).

19. M. S. Knowles & Associates, *Andragogy in Action: Applying Modern Principles of Adult Learning* (San Francisco: Jossey-Bass, 1985), 1.

20. Richard Badham and Pelle Ehn, "Tinkering with Technology: Human Factors, Work Redesign, and Professionals in Workplace Innovation," *Human Factors and Ergonomics in Manufacturing* 10, no. 1 (2000).

21. Bryce Allen, *Information Tasks: Toward a User-Centered Approach to Information Systems* (San Diego: Academic Press, 1996).

22. Donald A. Norman and Stephen W. Draper, eds., *User-Centered System Design: New Perspectives on Human-Computer Interaction* (Hillsdale, N.J.: Lawrence Erlbaum Associates, 1986).

23. Donald A. Norman, "Cognitive Engineering," in Norman and Draper, eds., *User-Centered System Design.*

24. Norman, "Cognitive Engineering," 32.

25. Norman, "Cognitive Engineering."

26. B. Allen, *Information Tasks.*

27. A. Dillon, *Designing Usable Electronic Text: Ergonomic Aspects of Human Information Usage* (London: Taylor and Francis, 1994).

28. G. M. Olson and G. S. Olson, "User-Centered Design of Collaboration Technology," *Journal of Organizational Computing* 1, no. 1 (1991).

29. D. E. Mahling, "Cognitive Systems Engineering for Visualization," in *Cognitive Aspects of Visual Languages and Visual Interfaces*, ed. M. J. Tauber, D. E. Mahling, and F. Arefi (Amsterdam: North-Holland).

30. Allen, *Information Tasks,* 25.

31. Allen, *Information Tasks,* 25.

32. Allen, *Information Tasks,* 26.

33. Nicholas J. Belkin and A. Vickery, *Interaction in Information Systems: A Review of Research from Document Retrieval to Knowledge-Based Systems*, Library and Information Research Report 35 (London: British Library, 1985); R. S. Taylor, "Question-Negotiation and Information Seeking in Libraries," *College and Research Libraries* 29, no. 3 (1968); G. Wersig, "The Problematic Situation as a Basic Concept of Information Science in the Framework of the Social Sciences: A Reply to Belkin," in *International Federation for Documentation: Theoretical Problems of Informatics* (Moscow: VINITI, 1979).

34. M. De Mey, "The Cognitive Viewpoint: Its Development and Its Scope," in *International Workshop on the Cognitive Viewpoint*, ed. M. De Mey (Ghent: University of Ghent, 1977); M. De Mey, *The Cognitive Paradigm* (Dordrecht: Reidel, 1982); Nicholas J. Belkin, "Cognitive Models and Information Transfer," *Social Science Information Studies* 4 (1984); P. Ingwersen, "Search Procedures in the Library, Analysed from the Cognitive Point of View," *Journal of Documentation* 38, no. 3 (1982); P. Ingwersen, "A Cognitive View of Three Selected Online Search Facilities," *Online Review* 8, no. 5 (1984); T. D. Wilson, "The Cognitive Approach to Information-Seeking Behavior and Information Use," *Social Science Information Studies* 4 (1984).

35. Belkin, "Cognitive Models and Information Transfer"; Peter Ingwersen, *Information Retrieval Interaction* (London: Taylor Graham, 1992).

36. Brenda Dervin and M. Nilan, "Information Needs and Uses," *Annual Review of Science and Technology* 21 (1986).

37. Carol Collier Kuhlthau, "Inside the Search Process: Information Seeking from the User's Perspective," *Journal of the American Society for Information Science* 42, no. 5 (1991).

38. D. Ellis, "The Physical and Cognitive Paradigms in Information Retrieval Research," *Journal of Documentation* 48, no. 1 (1992).

39. Dervin and Nilan, "Information Needs and Uses."

40. Ellis, "The Physical and Cognitive Paradigms in Information Retrieval Research."

41. Dervin and Nilan, "Information Needs and Uses."

42. Dervin and Nilan, "Information Needs and Uses," 16.

43. Tefko Saracevic et al., "A Study of Information Seeking and Retrieving, I: Background and Methodology," *Journal of the American Society for Information Science* 39, no. 3 (1988); Tefko Saracevic and Paul Kantor, "A Study of Information Seeking and Retrieving, II: Users, Questions, and Effectiveness," *Journal of the American Society for Information Science* 39, no. 3 (1988); Tefko Saracevic and Paul Kantor, "A Study of Information Seeking and Retrieving, III: Searchers, Searches, and Overlap," *Journal of the American Society for Information Science* 39, no. 3 (1988).

44. D. M. Barbuto and E. E. Cevallos, "End-User Searching: Program Review and Future Prospects," *Reference Quarterly* 31, no. 2 (1991); P. W. Dalrymple, "Retrieval by Reformulation in Two Library Catalogs: Towards a Cognitive Model of Searching Behavior," *Journal of the American Society for Information Science* 41, no. 4 (1990); Carol Collier Kuhlthau, Betty J. Turock, and Robert J. Belvin, "Facilitating Information Seeking through Cognitive Models of the Search Process" (paper presented at the 51st Annual Meeting of the American Society for Information Science, 1988); Kuhlthau, "Inside the Search Process."

45. N. J. Belkin, T. Seeger, and G. Wersig, "Distributed Expert Problem Treatment as a Model for Information System Analysis and Design," *Journal of Information Science* 5 (1983); N. J. Belkin et al., "Distributed Expert-Based Information Systems: An Interdisciplinary Approach," *Information Processing and Management* 23, no. 5 (1987); Christine L. Borgman, Donald Owen Case, and Charles T. Meadow, "Incorporating Users' Information Seeking Styles into the Design of an

Information Retrieval Interface" (paper presented at the 48th Annual Meeting of the Society for Information Science, 1985); C. L. Borgman, Donald Owen Case, and Charles T. Meadow, "The Design and Evaluation of a Front-End User Interface for Energy Researchers," *Journal of the American Society for Information Science* 40, no. 2 (1989); Hsinchun Chen and Vasant Dhar, "Cognitive Process as a Basis for Intelligent Retrieval Systems Design," *Information Processing and Management* 27, no. 5 (1991); W. Bruce Croft and R. H. Thompson, "I³R: A New Approach to the Design of Document Retrieval Systems," *Journal of the American Society for Information Science* 38, no. 6 (1987); Gregory B. Newby, "User Models in Information Retrieval: Applying Knowledge about Human Communication to Computer Interface Design" (paper presented at the 52d Annual Meeting of the American Society for Information Science, 1989).

46. Howard Beales et al., "Consumer Search and Public Policy," *Journal of Consumer Research* 8 (1981); David H. Furse, Girish N. Punj, and David W. Stewart, "A Typology of Individual Search Strategies among Purchases of New Automobiles," *Journal of Consumer Research* 10 (1984).

47. D. Halpern and M. Nilan, "A Step toward Shifting the Research Emphasis in Information Science from the System to the User: An Empirical Investigation of Source-Evaluation Behaviour Information Seeking and Use" (paper presented at the 51st Annual Meeting of the American Society for Information Science, 1988); J. W. Janes, "Relevance Judgments and the Incremental Presentation of Document Presentations," *Information Processing and Management* 27, no. 6 (1991); M. Eisenberg and L. Schamber, "Relevance: The Search for a Definition" (paper presented at the 51st Annual Meeting of the American Society for Information Science, 1988); Harry Bruce, "A Cognitive View of the Situational Dynamism of User-Centered Relevance Estimation," *Journal of the American Society for Information Science* 45, no. 3 (1994).

48. E. T. Hewins, "Information Need and Use Studies," *Annual Review of Science and Technology* 25 (1990).

49. N. J. Belkin, "The Cognitive Viewpoint in Information Science," *Journal of Information Science* 16 (1990).

50. Belkin, "The Cognitive Viewpoint in Information Science," 11-12.

51. De Mey, *The Cognitive Paradigm*, 4.

52. Belkin, "The Cognitive Viewpoint in Information Science," 14-15.

53. E.g., D. Ellis, "A Behavioural Approach to Information System Design," *Journal of Documentation* 45, no. 3 (1989); Kulthau, "Inside the Search Process"; Pamela E. Sandstrom, "An Optimal Foraging Approach to Information Seeking and Use," *Library Quarterly* 64, no. 4 (1994).

54. M. E. Brown, "A General Model of Information-Seeking Behavior" (paper presented at the 54th Annual Meeting of the American Society for Information Science, 1991).

55. Karen Pettigrew, Raya Fidel, and Harry Bruce, "Conceptual Frameworks in Information Behavior," *Annual Review of Information Science and Technology* 35 (2001).

56. Raya Fidel and Efthimis Efthimiadis. "Content Organization and Retrieval Project, Phase I: A Work-Centered Examination of Web Searching Behavior of Boeing Engineers." (Seattle: Boeing Company, 1998).

57. Henry Jay Becker, "Internet Use by Teachers: Conditions of Professional Use and Teacher-Directed Student Use" (Irvine, Calif.: Center for Research on Information Technology and Organizations, 1999); Lisa Hack and Sue Smey, "A Survey of Internet Use by Teachers in Three Urban Connecticut Schools," *School Library Media Quarterly* 25, no. 3 (1997); Phillip J. Vanfossen, "Degree of Internet/WWW Use and Barriers to Use among Secondary Social Studies Teachers," *International Journal of Instructional Media* 28, no. 1 (2001); Randall L. Wiesenmayer and George R. Meadows, "Addressing Science Teachers' Initial Perceptions of the Classroom Uses of Internet and World Wide Web-Based Resource Materials," *Journal of Science Education and Technology* 6, no. 4 (1997).

58. Karen Pettigrew, "Lay Information Provision in Community Settings: How Community Health Nurses Disseminate Human Services Information to the Elderly," *Library Quarterly* 70, no. 1 (2000).

59. Andrelyn Applebee et al., *Academics Online: A Nationwide Quantitative Study of Australian Academic Use of the Internet* (Adelaide, Australia: Auslib Press, 1998); Harry Bruce, "Perceptions of the Internet: What People Think of When They Search the Internet for Information," *Internet Research: Electronic Networking Applications and Policy* 9, no. 3 (1999); Susan S. Lazinger, Judit Bar-Ilan, and Bluma C. Peritz, "Internet Use by Faculty Members in Various Disciplines: A Comparative Case Study," *Journal of the American Society for Infor-*

mation Science 48, no. 6 (1997); Peter Liebscher, Eileen G. Abels, and Daniel W. Denman, "Factors That Influence the Use of Electronic Networks by Science and Engineering Faculty at Small Institutions, Part II: Preliminary Use Indicators," *Journal of the American Society for Information Science* 48, no. 6 (1997); Henk J. Voorbij, "Searching Scientific Information on the Internet: A Dutch Academic User Survey," *Journal of the American Society for Information Science* 50, no. 7 (1999).

60. Reijo Savolainen, "Everyday Life Information Seeking: Approaching Information Seeking in the Context of Way of Life," *Library and Information Science Research* 17, no. 3 (1995).

61. Brenda Dervin, "On Studying Information Seeking Methodologically: The Implications of Connecting Metatheory to Method," *Information Processing and Management* 35, no. 6 (1999).

62. Sanna Talja, "Constituting 'Information' and 'User' as Research Objects: A Theory of Knowledge Formations as an Alternative to the Information Man-Theory" (paper presented at the Information Seeking in Context Conference, Tampere, Finland, August 14-16, 1996).

63. Raymond Williams, *Marxism and Literature* (Oxford: Oxford University Press, 1977).

64. Talja, "Constituting 'Information' and 'User' as Research Objects."

65. Talja, "Constituting 'Information' and 'User' as Research Objects."

66. Bruno Latour, *Pandora's Hope: Essays on the Reality of Science Studies* (Cambridge, Mass.: Harvard University Press, 1999).

67. Brenda Dervin, "Information Needs and Information Seeking: The Search for Questions behind the Research Agenda," (paper presented at the UCLA-NSF Workshop on Social Aspects of Digital Libraries, Los Angeles, 1996).

68. Latour, *Pandora's Hope*, 69.

69. Dervin, "Information Needs and Information Seeking."

Chapter 4

Users of the Internet

The evolution of the Internet appearing in chapter 1 of this book described the end-user provenance and development of the Internet. In chapter 2 and 3 the theoretical tools for our analysis of the Internet were introduced. With this background in place, we now face a number of key questions. Who are Internet users? What do we know about how and why people use the Internet? What does Internet using tell us about the Internet?

The first step toward answering these questions and building the theories and constructs that comprise the user's view of the Internet is to examine the research data that describe people using the Internet. It must first be emphasized that we are telling the Internet story from the perspective of the Internet user. There are many people around the world who do not, or cannot, use the Internet for a range of economic, social, geographic, and cultural reasons. Their story is an important aspect of the Internet story and is critical to issues such as the digital divide, universal service, equity, national sovereignty, and global information infrastructure, but our focus is not on nonuse where the choice does not belong with the individual. We are telling the story of the Internet and building constructions of the Internet from the user's perspective. To explicate this view, we will be synthesizing data from the many and varied research studies that have focused upon Internet users in modern economies around the world from Australia and Asia to Africa, the Middle East, Europe, Canada, and Mexico. The story of the Internet began in the

United States, so our review also includes many studies of Internet users from this country. The studies selected for this synthesis come from a range of disciplines but predominantly those that are associated with the information field. In general, this research has been conducted within the extant construct of users, contexts, and systems with a focus on users rather than usings. Our description of the research data is therefore directed by this structure, but the reader is urged to hear the stories of people using the Internet that appear in the data. In chapter 5 we will elaborate the theory that is grounded in this data—the theory that gives rise to the user's view of the Internet.

Our review begins with research on Internet users in professional roles—academics, librarians, and teachers. We then discuss Internet use by the younger generation—college students, youths, and young adults. Next, the review moves to research that focuses on users of specific Internet services—government information and e-commerce. Finally, our review examines research that describes the general public as users of the Internet.

Use of the Internet by Academics

It makes sense to begin our discussion of Internet use with academics because this group arguably includes the first beneficiaries of Internet development and innovation. Certainly, academics, scholars, and faculty members have been the most long-term users of Internet resources. Even as recently as 1991, the primary users of the World Wide Web were a small network of university researchers.[1]

Academic Internet users have been studied and observed extensively since the development of the network because the initial rhetoric that formulated various constructions of benefit to be derived from network technologies focused on the usings of researchers, scholars, and teachers from the academic sector.[2] Indeed, the ARPA experiment described in chapter 1 was a research project used by researchers and scholars. The NSFNet was also initially set up with the goal of facilitating resource sharing among academic researchers who were recipients of NSF funding. Many of the early information provision and dissemination initiatives of library and scholarly communications professionals were also formulated with the needs and requirements of the academic sector in mind.

Academics have, therefore, been involved with the Internet from its inception, and this group of Internet users has been a primary focus of many studies. As a result, we know a lot about academic users of the Internet. We know how much this group of professionals is using the Internet. We know about the way Internet resources are being used to facilitate aspects of the academic role. We know about the attitude that academics have toward the Internet and Internet tools. We know about the role the Internet plays in supporting the work of academics and where it fits in with the facilities and tools that academics use to perform work-related tasks.

Research that examines how and why academics are using the Internet has taken different forms, applied various methods and approaches, and explored many different samples of people working in the academic sector in numerous countries, regions, and locations. The most common methods for collecting data for studies of academics using the Internet have been written surveys and questionnaires distributed either by regular or electronic mail.[3] Some studies have combined written surveys with interviews,[4] or conducted a structured interview with academics in the research sample, face to face[5] or via the telephone.[6] Studies have also collected data by leaving questionnaires beside Internet terminals for participants to fill in.[7] Most research has been designed around single case studies; longitudinal studies are rare.[8]

Frequency of Internet Use

The number of academics using the Internet has been constantly increasing with the ongoing development of network services and the installation and support of Internet facilities on university campuses. The funding for Internet infrastructure is generally justified by assumptions that relate using the services of the network with enhanced academic productivity. Academics are, therefore, actively encouraged to use the Internet in their work.

Recent international studies[9] and research in the United States[10] report that about three-quarters of academics describe themselves as users of the Internet. These figures reflect what academics perceive when asked if they use the Internet and probably reflect a lower level of use than is actually the case. Some academics do not regard themselves as users of the Internet because they are not experts or do not use the network regularly or in innovative or novel ways. There is also evidence that some academics are confused about what "using the Internet" actually means. In early studies,[11] when academics were asked if they were using the Internet, some declared that they thought they were using the network but were not sure if this was the case. This confusion may still arise, because Internet infrastructure is becoming increasingly transparent in the academic setting. Most academics have a computer in their office connected to the Internet.[12]

Academics, therefore, have access to the Internet at work but they are also very likely to have access to the network in their homes. Data on home access vary but some studies[13] report up to 95 percent of faculty having Internet access at home. For other studies,[14] this figure is lower, showing home access to Internet resources up to one-third lower than access to the Internet at work.

The actual proportion of academics using the Internet varies according to the sample of academics studied. From the numerous studies consulted for this review it is clear, however, that large numbers of academics are using the Internet. They are also using the Internet frequently. In some studies almost all academics surveyed report that they were using the Internet at least once a week and nearly one-half indicate that they use the network on a daily basis.[15] This frequency of use is confirmed in other studies that report more than three-quarters of academics accessing the Internet more regularly than once a week.[16] In fact, academics may be using the Internet on average as much as twenty hours per week.[17] Academics from different disciplines use the Internet with varying frequencies[18] and for different purposes.[19] This is generally explained by differential network resource allocation. Some academic disciplines in some universities lack appropriate network resources.[20]

Reasons for Not Using the Internet

With such widespread use of the Internet by academics, it is interesting to examine the reasons that some academics give for *not* using the Internet. Predominantly, nonuse has been explained by lack of access to the right facilities. Some nonusers complain of a lack of access to a workstation or the need to share a workstation with others.[21] Another explanation for not using the Internet is that some academics still lack confidence in their own ability to use the network and its resources effectively. Again, this is both supported[22] and contradicted[23] by research, but it is common for academics to underrate their skills with technology. Overall, perceived ease of use is not a key factor influencing adoption of, and use of, the Internet by academics,[24] but several studies have found that academics are inclined to report themselves as beginner rather than competent or expert users of the network.[25] Many academics are disinclined to accept the mantle of "technology expert." The designation of expert can put people "on the spot" in an academic environment, and there are some disciplines where this designation may be expected (computer science) and others where it might be regarded as extraordinary or out of character (medieval studies).

Length of Internet Use

Academics have been using the Internet for longer than any other group of users. Many Internet innovations have evolved from academics wanting to use the network or its resources in particular ways. A high proportion of academics are, therefore, long-term users of the Internet and experienced users of computers in general.[26] A recent study, for example, reports that nearly half of the academics surveyed had been using the Internet for five to nine years. This study also reveals that slightly more than one-quarter of the academics in the sample had been using the Internet for ten to fourteen years and 12.3 percent had been using the Internet for over fifteen years.[27] These figures are supported by data from earlier studies reporting nearly one-third of academics having used the Internet for more than seven years.[28] Length of Internet use can depend on the discipline in which an academic is working; scientists and social scientists have been using the Internet longer than humanists, for example.[29]

How Academics Use the Internet

The Internet usings of academics have been the focus of numerous research studies in countries such as the United States,[30] Australia,[31] the Netherlands,[32] Canada,[33] Israel,[34] and Wales.[35] In most cases, this research examines Internet use by academics in relation to the roles of teaching, research, publication, contribution to a discipline and professional community, and administration. In research by the author,[36] for example, the using of a range of Internet services (email, remote login, newsgroups, FTP) by academics to support these various roles was elaborated:

> Academics use email for:
>
> Research
> - To keep up to date with developments occurring in research in their discipline
> - To facilitate collaborative research
> - To overcome geographic remoteness
>
> Teaching
> - To maintain current awareness and exchange ideas with colleagues
> - To facilitate cross-campus communication

- To improve honors and higher degree supervision

Publication
- To facilitate collaboration
- To accelerate the speed of submission and refereeing of publications

Administration
- To facilitate committee work
- To improve the administration of departments
- To facilitate administrative functions across campuses, across institutions, and at an international level

Contribution to the discipline, profession, or industry
- To facilitate a sense of disciplinary collegiality
- To organize conferences
- To arrange study leave, job exchanges, and attendance at overseas conferences
- To facilitate collaboration with industry

Academics use remote login for:

Research
- To gain access to more powerful computing facilities
- To facilitate reciprocated access between research collaborators
- To obtain access to library catalogues and databases used in research
- To obtain access to discipline specific databases

Teaching
- To obtain access to library catalogues
- To obtain access to discussion groups

- To facilitate problem solving for advanced degree supervision

Publication
- To verify bibliographic details, undertake literature searches, and check what has been published in a particular area

Administration
- To obtain access to student records

Academics use newsgroups for:

Research
- To obtain current awareness
- To obtain solutions for specific problems

Teaching
- To facilitate an exchange of ideas
- To obtain information about computer programs used for teaching
- To obtain ideas for lectures and tutorials

Publication
- To access conference calls for papers
- To promote publication interests

Administration
- To place job advertisements
- To overcome problems with software

Contribution to the discipline, profession, industry
- To assist fellow academics
- To access debate in the discipline

Academics use FTP for:

Research
- To obtain software suitable for research projects
- To exchange data with research collaborators

Teaching
- To obtain software for teaching purposes

Publication
- To facilitate publication
- To obtain publication techniques

Administration
- To facilitate committee work
- Contribution to the discipline, profession, or industry
- To disseminate ideas[37]

Of all Internet services, email is certainly the focus of academic use of the Internet. The majority of academics find email either useful or very useful for administration, for research, for communicating with colleagues as part of the teaching process, for personal use, for publication, for communicating with students as part of the teaching process, and for community service and contributions to the profession or industry.[38] Academics regard email as very useful[39] and the most important Internet service.[40] This is verified in numerous studies showing nearly all academics surveyed using email[41] on a daily basis[42] and rating it the most important Internet service. Indeed, academics can spend nearly twice as much time per week using email as opposed to other services.[43] Studies show that most academics send and receive between one and twenty messages in a typical workweek and more than a third either send or receive more than twenty messages,[44] meaning that using email may account for more than seven hours per week for most academics.[45]

Academics are therefore using email a lot and frequently, but what does this actually mean? What are academics *doing* with email? The author's early research associated the uses of email with various academic roles (as described above),[46] and this has since been confirmed by more recent studies that associate use of email with academics making contact with research collaborators or at least declaring that their use of email is directly related to their researching.[47] There are reports that academics use email a lot for social purposes,[48] but this may be more an artifact of academic collegial networks and the demands of maintaining links with fellow academics. The academic role is very much tied to the affiliation and affirmation that scholarly networks provide and the use of email to augment an academic's capacity to make contact with those who share a research interest and research agenda is often confused with social rather than work-related outcomes.

Studies reveal that academics do not associate their email using with the roles they perform as a teacher,[49] but in recent years, academics have certainly been using email to make contact with students, for the submission of assignments, and for the transfer of content and instructions. In the earlier years of the Internet, the infrastructures in academic settings were more supportive of faculty in the academic community than students. This is definitely not the case any more. Campuses now extensively support student email services and academics are increasingly finding email an effective way to enhance their teaching. Earlier studies that identified academics reporting the usefulness of file transfer (FTP) for teaching[50] in a way predicted this trend. A common use of email by faculty is to attach files that are then transferred to a cohort or class through an email list.

Using Discussion Lists

As noted, networking and collegiality are important dimensions of academic life. Not surprisingly, a significant proportion of academics use email for discussion group interactions with colleagues and students[51] at least once per week.[52] The volume and frequency of discussion list use can vary across disciplines.[53] In some studies, researchers distinguish using email and using discussion groups[54] because academic Internet users of the late 1980s and early 1990s participated in discussions across newsgroups. Most contemporary discussion lists, however, are mounted as email listservs. It can therefore be difficult for academics responding to a researcher's questions about discussion groups to separate use of these discussion lists from email use. Many academics are members of numerous lists, which connect them to discussions about their discipline, research interests, professional associations, and so on. Many academics also host email lists associated with a course they are teaching or a committee they are chairing.

Clearly, academics find discussion lists useful. The academic role is characterized by affiliation with a discipline and the critical acceptance of new knowledge generated by research and scholarship. Academics need to gather and disseminate information. Communication channels are therefore crucial to all aspects of academic work. Academics find discussion lists useful for their research activities and teaching.[55] This is not to say that they consider discussion groups a substitute for other sources of professional information. Internet discussion lists are good, but most academics do not see them as a replacement for more traditional forms of professional engagement such as conferences, lecture series, and workshops.[56] There are some indications that we may see more specific uses of discussion lists by academics in the future because junior faculty are using discussion lists to support teaching and publication more than senior faculty.[57]

Electronic Journal Use

One of the features of the rhetoric that has surrounded Internet use by the academic community is the potential for what some call the emergence of an "electronic culture" of scholarship. This refers to the digital creation and dissemination of scholarly output. Certainly, university administrators and university librarians have taken a keen interest in the likelihood of this transformation and the impact that this will have on library budgets and scholarly publishing. The publication of electronic journals has been fairly widespread but in the academic sector, at least, this form of publication is not yet flourishing. The academic community lives by the rules of tenure, and widespread acceptance of the legitimacy of peer-reviewed electronic publication has not yet been established as a substitute for the traditional print-based, peer-assessed scholarly journal as the premier form for disseminating new knowledge in most disciplines. Many hybrid journals exist in both print and electronic form. Most electronic journals are little more that a digitized version of the printed form. There is a widespread interest in how we might transform the dissemination of new knowledge by comprehensive exploitation of the versatility of digitized text and image. The document in digital form can speak to the reader in a very individual way, providing links to real data, flexible forms of information in text and image, video and audio, citation trails, searchability, and so on.

There is some indication that more widespread acceptance of electronic publication is occurring faster for some academic disciplines such as physics than for disciplines such as English and psychology,[58] but the same research also indicates that only a small proportion of academics are subscribing to electronic journals[59] and a majority of academics do not consult electronic journals on a regular basis.[60] There is, of course, a set of literacies that academics must acquire before widespread acceptance and use of electronic journals is likely. Many academics feel that they do not have sufficient experience to evaluate the quality of electronic journals.[61] Confidence in the credibility and the long-term viability of e-journals as a vehicle for dissemination of new knowledge is vital. Most academics have developed their scholarship and a respect for their discipline through traditional channels of scholarly dissemination. They know how to judge this medium. Academics need to learn how to evaluate the qualities of an electronic journal in the way they evaluate the qualities of a print-based journal.

An overriding concern is the stability of electronic forms of publishing. Peer-reviewed, print-based journals have been not only a vehicle for dissemination but also an important archival format for the knowledge base of most academic disciplines. There will be no widespread shift to electronic publishing in most academic disciplines until academics are certain that digital formats will provide long-lasting, searchable, reliable, credible, and browsable information repositories. Research indicates that academics are expressing concern about the quality of electronic journals and the loss of the browsing capacity that they have with print-based publications.[62] Academics would like electronic sources to be more reliable, of better quality, better organized, and more stable.[63]

Use of World Wide Web/Searching on the Web

The Internet innovations that have most affected academic use of the network are, without doubt, the development of the World Wide Web (WWW) and graphics-based browsers. These developments have made the resources of the Internet more accessible and have arguably increased the number of users of the Internet and the characteristics of Internet use. Clearly, academics are using the WWW regularly. A majority of academics are using Web browsers on a daily basis, and almost all faculty appear to be using the Web at least once per week.[64]

Academic use of the WWW is most often associated with searches for information. Academics are either trying to locate information on a topic by searching the Internet, linking to a known site or information resource that they have located previously, or linking to a site that has been recommended by a colleague or referenced through their personal information network. Searching the WWW for information is common. A majority of academics report using search engines and the Web to locate information two or three times a week[65] or at least occasionally.[66] Indeed, a large proportion of academics use the WWW in this way every day.[67]

Use of Other Internet Services

Of course, academics are using other Internet services apart from email and the WWW. There have been numerous studies that have explored the uses of file transfer, remote databases, run programs, and Netnews. Obviously, the applications and intensity of use of these services varies.

File transfer is a relatively popular Internet service for academics. Studies reveal that many academics are using the Internet to transfer files[68] perhaps as regularly as two or three times a week.[69] Access to online databases is also common.[70] Studies have found that more than three-quarters of the academics surveyed are using online databases at least once per week to support their teaching and research.[71]

Learning How to Use the Internet

Research clearly indicates that academics learn how to use Internet resources, services, and tools either by some form of self-instruction and trial and error or by seeking the assistance of a close colleague. There are some differences in this trend among academics from various disciplines, with science academics slightly more likely to have learned how to use the Internet without any formal training than humanities and social science scholars. But for both broad categories, the trend is clearly toward self-instruction.[72] Most academics have never attended any form of Internet training course.[73] In general, the academics that choose to attend training sessions are those who consider themselves less experienced with the network and its services. Academics who consider themselves to be knowledgeable in the use of the network do not attend training.[74]

In a study by the author,[75] which aimed to tap into what was referred to as a "heightened awareness of the benefits of Internet use to the academic role," participants were recruited from academics who were enrolled in Internet training courses. Overwhelmingly, this sampling frame represented people who were nonusers or novice users of the Internet. Academics were not enrolling in the Internet training course to acquire advanced-level skills. This analysis was confirmed in later studies by the author aimed at examining a relationship between satisfaction with information seeking on the Internet and variables like training. This research found no significant difference in either the behaviors or the levels of satisfaction with information seeking between academics who had attended an Internet training course and those who had not.[76]

Factors Affecting Internet Use by Academics

There have been a number of attempts not only to describe the use of the Internet by academics but also to identify factors that affect the way an academic might use the services and resources of the network. Demographic factors such as age, sex, income, and education have been related to academic use of the Internet. Not surprisingly, younger males tend to be heavier users of the Internet. Income and education are not significant predictors of Internet use, but heavier users of the Internet are also those who tend to own more advanced forms of technology.[77]

Certain factors related to the way academics perceive the Internet have also been found to affect Internet use. The way an academic perceives his or her level of Internet experience can be correlated with the number of services used and the frequency of that use. There is also a strong correlation between perceived utility of the Internet and use variables. This means that increased use of the Internet (using more services in a more intensive manner) is correlated with seeing the Internet as a useful tool.[78] Heavier users of the Internet tend to be academics that have a positive perception of the Internet on two levels. These academics see the Internet as less complex and have a more positive view of the advantages of Internet use.[79] The academics that have been using the network for a longer time are also those who are using a larger number of services in a more intense way.[80]

How frequently an academic uses the Internet to search for information has also been related to search preferences and patterns. Research has shown that more-frequent searchers are more likely to use search engines and that academics who search the Internet less frequently are more likely to use online databases.[81]

Not surprisingly, studies have also revealed that the level of an academic's Internet experience is related to the intensity of the academic's Internet use. There is a positive correlation between years of Internet experience and the number of hours a person is likely to be online.[82] Experience and ease of use relate significantly to the number of services used and the intensity of Internet use.[83]

Information Seeking on the Internet

Academic usings of the Internet, in general, characterize the network as an information environment or a communication infrastructure. Most academics use the Internet for affiliation, affirmation, and information.

Academics are keen to use the Internet for information seeking. This is not to say that they are necessarily expert at searching for the information they need or that they have a high opinion of the Internet as an information source or medium for accessing the information sources they want to use.

Studies of information searching on the Internet by academics reveal that faculty members have mixed feelings about the Internet as an information source. They enjoy the advantages of Internet information searching but also acknowledge a range of shortcomings.[84] The biggest concern for academics is the large number of irrelevant hits from their searches. Academics also complain about the lack of quality in the resources that are located on the Internet,[85] although, as noted earlier, there is some doubt about the ability of many academics to judge the authenticity of certain Internet resources. In spite of this, research shows that as many as one-third of academics consider subject searches on the Internet easy and approximately two-thirds claim that search results justify or strongly justify the searching time.[86]

Academics tend to be satisfied with their searches for information on the Internet.[87] This may be explained by the fact that academics generally have lots of experience gathering information in their respective disciplines. They have also spent many hours following citation trails and searching for obscure information sources. Tools that streamline these processes or connect an academic with information sources from a desktop (at the point of need) improve the efficiencies of scholarship and are regarded favorably.

These are perceptions, of course, and some studies have attempted to tap into the way academics perceive the Internet when they are using the network to search for information. What is revealed by these studies is that academics, like many users of the Internet or information systems in general, tend to perceive what they are doing as analogous to some more commonplace or everyday activity. Studies of online database use, for example, have revealed the metaphor of "going fishing" for information.[88] A recent study of academics using the Internet explored this notion and found that there are a number of dominant metaphors that academics use when they search the Internet for information and that these metaphors are related to the degree of satisfaction that academics derive from information seeking on the Internet.

The study found that there are two common ways that academics perceive the Internet. First, they may conceptualize the Internet with an emphasis on information, information storage, and access to information, seeing the Internet like a library or a databank. Second, they may conceptualize the Internet structurally, emphasizing connectivity and networking. The study found that academics that conceptualize the Internet as an information store or library have higher levels of satisfaction with information seeking on the Internet than academics that conceptualize the Internet as a structure of connectivity and interconnectedness.[89] Further exploration of the satisfaction that academics derive from information seeking on the Internet also revealed that there is no significant difference between the amount of satisfaction with information seeking derived by academics who regard themselves as frequent information searchers on the Internet and those who regard themselves as infrequent searchers. The results do indicate, however, that academics who have a higher expectation of success when they search the Internet for information will also express higher levels of satisfaction with information seeking and searching on the Internet.

Use of the Internet by Librarians

A second group of foundation stakeholders and long-term users of the Internet are librarians. Among the first information services to be attached to the Internet were the Online Public Access Catalog (OPAC) systems of university libraries. Some of the first high-end users of the Internet were therefore the librarians who built and administered these systems. Librarians also played a role in setting the agendas for infrastructure development for the local campuses and regional information networks that underpinned the early developments of the Internet. Also, many of the values of library practice such as open access, collaboration, and information at the point of need became the underlying principles of early internetworking and, over time, have affected the evolving character of the network.

It has been claimed that the Internet is changing the nature of libraries and the role of librarians. Some posit there will be little need for the institution and/or the principles and practices of library in our digital future. Others claim that we need librarians and libraries now more than ever before. Whichever is the case, there can be little argument with the proposition that the Internet has transformed librarianship and libraries. The way librarians are using the Internet will certainly shape the user's view of the Internet.

Studies of the use of the Internet by librarians have collected data using questionnaires,[90] structured interviews,[91] and a combination of questionnaire and interview methods.[92]

Acceptance of the Internet

Research leaves little doubt that the majority of librarians are using the Internet on a regular basis to perform their work roles.

In fact, there is a strong acceptance of the Internet in the professional lives of librarians.[93] Most regard the Internet is either essential or useful[94] to their work. Clearly, the Internet connects library professionals with many information services and resources that they need to do their jobs, but in many cases the work of librarians is now designated as the collecting and organizing of digital resources that will be accessed via the Internet. There is some variation in the levels of use and nonuse of the Internet by librarians, depending on the type of library in which a librarian works. Academic librarians are reportedly the most frequent users of the Internet.[95] School librarians are the next most likely to be active users of the Internet, with high proportions of these professionals using the network in relation to their work tasks.[96] This is followed by business librarians,[97] and then information professionals in the banking and finance industry.[98]

In fact, it has become such a common assumption that librarians are using the Internet on a regular basis that the proportions of Internet use/nonuse have become a moot point for many researchers. If librarians have access to the Internet, they are assumed to be using the network to perform the functions of their job, but access for librarians does vary according to the location of the library. Less than three-quarters of librarians in a study of libraries in Sub-Saharan Africa, for example, have access to full Internet services.[99] By contrast, nearly all reference librarians in academic libraries in the United States have access to the Internet at the reference desk.[100] In Canada, one study at least indicates that around 60 percent of librarians have "ready access" to the Internet while 40 percent do not.[101]

Frequency of Internet Use

In the same way, the frequency of a librarian's Internet use may depend on the type of library in which the professional is working and also the role that the librarian is performing. Studies show that slightly more than one-third of librarians are online two to three times a week, one-third are online one to two hours per day, and slightly more than one-tenth are online more than two hours per day.[102] Legal information professionals may spend more than five hours per week on the Internet,[103] and law librarians are using the Internet on a daily basis.[104]

Frequency of use also depends on the Internet service being used. Email is the most popular Internet service for librarians. Studies confirm that librarians are spending about one-quarter of the time that they are online doing email.[105] Mailing lists are also very popular among librarians; most librarians belong to at least one mailing list.[106] As a professional group, librarians have active networks that function to keep practitioners up to date. These networks are also active because the primary role of a librarian is information provision. This often involves complex collaborations and resource sharing, and it stands to reason that mailing lists and interest group discussion are a popular application of the Internet for this professional group. Some librarians can also feel isolated professionally. Librarians in regional libraries or in remote locations can be the only professional working in their institution. It is not surprising that librarians report that professional networking, personal communication, and participation in discussion groups are the most important reasons for using the Internet.[107]

Librarians also spend a significant amount of time on the World Wide Web. Studies indicate that librarians are spending about one-third of their Internet time using features of the WWW[108] and consider that accessing Web pages is one of the most important uses of the Internet.[109] Librarians are using the WWW to access information about professional organizations, electronic journals, and virtual conference sites.[110]

The most popular application of the Internet for librarians after email and the WWW is the use of library catalogs (OPACs).[111] As mentioned previously, librarians played a significant role in the establishment of the information infrastructure of the Internet through the development and administration of local information services that were ultimately attached to the Internet. The most fundamental of these information services was the library catalog. Today, Internet users have access to library catalogs around the world, and the most stable and reliable information sources on the Internet are found at these sites. Information networking and resource sharing are basic, long-term values of librarianship. Facilitating access to other library catalogs and thereby expanding the resource base for local users of libraries and reference services is a very important using of the Internet by librarians.

Librarians use the Internet primarily for reference and research. Studies report that a majority of librarians are using the Internet for reference frequently and perhaps as many as a third are using the Internet for this purpose very frequently.[112] Use of the Internet for reference and research often depends on whether the librarian has access to the network at the reference desk[113] and whether he or she considers the information needed represents a "serious" reference question.[114] Librarians are, of course, very sophisticated users of information sources and resources. They are able to distinguish the information values in Internet information services and show a preference for searching value-added databases on the Internet as opposed to simply using a Web search engine.[115]

Reasons for Nonuse

The main reason a librarian would *not* be using the Internet is if the library in which they work does not have access to the network.[116] Another reason given by librarians for not using the Internet relates to technical problems that are encountered and the frustration that this causes.[117] Many librarians have not been trained to manage network technologies, though this is changing rapidly due to the obvious demands on this type of professional expertise within the library setting. In fact, studies reveal that librarians with higher professional qualifications possess better Internet skills.[118]

Factors Affecting Internet Use by Librarians

Like other using groups, there are a number of factors that researchers have studied which affect the way librarians are using the Internet. For example, studies have shown that librarians over the age of fifty are slightly less likely to use the Internet for reference services. Not surprisingly, computer experience is also a factor. Librarians with computer proficiencies are more likely to be heavy users of the Internet.[119] In particular, this appears to be the case for librarians who are engaged in reference work.[120] Knowledge about the Internet in particular, as opposed to information technology in general, also affects Internet use by librarians. This knowledge may be the most important factor affecting Internet use by librarians. Librarians with a lot of knowledge about the Internet not only are more positively disposed to the Internet in an overall sense but also use more Internet tools and use them more frequently than librarians with little Internet knowledge.[121]

Working within a supportive environment is also an important factor that can enhance Internet use by librarians.[122] Like most professionals, librarians engage with a community of practitioners within and outside the workplace. They operate within a local professional environment that will ultimately affect the tools they choose for information provision. Not surprisingly, research reveals a direct relationship between collaboration with colleagues in the workplace and the number of hours per day that a librarian will access the Internet. Librarians who are alone in their Internet use access the network less each week than those who collaborate with other coworkers who also use the Internet.[123] This factor is a better predictor of Internet use by librarians than levels of personal innovativeness. In fact, it has been found that, for librarians, higher levels of innovativeness do not necessarily predict higher levels of usage of the Internet or the number of Internet tools that a librarian will use.[124]

Personal innovativeness does predict a more positive overall attitude toward the Internet, however, and attitude toward using the Internet, in a more general sense, does have an impact on the way librarians use the Internet. Generally, people tend to respond positively to technologies when their overall knowledge of the technology is high. This is the case for librarians and the Internet, where greater amounts of knowledge predict a more positive overall attitude toward the network and its applications in the professional environment. In fact, this becomes a self-supporting cycle for librarians. Feeling good about the Internet enhances the propensity to acquire knowledge about the network, and this new knowledge in turn positively influences the using of the Internet by librarians.[125]

It is interesting therefore to examine how librarians perceive their level of Internet skill. In general, librarians tend to be fairly modest in reporting their expertise using the Internet. This is not uncommon in other professional groups (like the academics discussed previously) and is probably manifest for the same reasons. Librarians are very aware of the transforming Internet and the pressing need to keep abreast of new developments. This places a burden of time and a commitment for regular use and review of new Internet innovations that most librarians cannot afford in their busy professional schedules. Studies indicate that these factors affect the confidence level that librarians have with using the Internet.[126] It is common for librarians to consider themselves competent rather than expert users of the Internet.[127]

Benefits and Problems Associated with Internet Use

As a professional group, librarians have been long-term champions of Internet development. Their advocacy set the agenda for establishing the base-level infrastructures and many of the information standards and protocols that underpin the Internet. It is not surprising, therefore, that studies of librarians using the Internet also focus on the way members of this profession express the benefits and problems associated with Internet use.

Librarians have positive views about using the Internet for communication[128]—in particular, professional communication. Librarians see the Internet as a vehicle for facilitating their professional networks. They seek professional affiliation and affirmation through their communication behaviors on the Internet. Opportunities for professional growth through electronic networking are second only to sharing information as the major benefit that librarians see deriving from their Internet use.[129] They see this benefit at a professional level but also at a client service level.[130]

Enhanced access to information not otherwise available is obviously the number one reason why librarians use the Internet and the primary benefit that they associate with Internet use. Librarians are conscious of the enhanced qualities of information provision that arise as a result of access to information sources on the Internet.[131] In particular, this means information that would otherwise not be available to the users of a particular library. The number one reason that librarians in recent studies claim for using the Internet is the enhancement of client services through the provision of information that would otherwise not be available at their home institution.[132] The Internet is reinforcing a perception of the library as a bridge to information rather than simply an information archive.[133] This includes a perception that the information on the Internet is also up to date.[134] Many of the information resources and services accessed through the Internet may not otherwise be available to library patrons because of limited library budgets; many librarians therefore see using the Internet as a way to access low-cost or free information sources.[135]

Librarians have a perception that using the Internet has enhanced their productivity. This perception of enhanced productivity is often related to qualities of specific service—in particular, reference services[136]—but it can also be associated with the speed of service.[137]

Librarians are, of course, very discerning users of the Internet, particularly in terms of the information dimensions of the network. They are very concerned about the quality and reliability of information on the Internet.[138] One recent study, for example, found that librarians were concerned that information available though the Internet is less authentic, reliable, and accurate.[139] Other studies find librarians questioning the volume and reliability of Internet information sources,[140] stating that the quality and accuracy of the information available on the Internet is not of a sufficiently high standard.[141] This is associated with librarians viewing the information on the Internet as disorganized.[142] One of the key features of librarianship is the expertise these practitioners have in the area of knowledge organization and representation. The field of librarianship has a distinguished record of keeping the artifacts of human knowledge and creativity organized for access. It stands to reason that librarians should criticize the lack of organization of information on the Internet.

Other criticisms of the Internet by librarians resolve around technical issues. Just keeping up with the technology is a problem that librarians perceive very strongly,[143] but the most common specific complaint with the Internet is that librarians perceive it as too slow.[144] Much of this criticism falls to the type of connection that a particular library facility might have. Studies, for example, reveal that many libraries have poor telecommunication facilities, high communication charges,[145] and a range of connection problems,[146] which inevitably influence a librarian's perception of the Internet. Technical issues associated with security are also major concerns for librarians.[147]

Internet Training

Librarians do feel a professional obligation to be knowledgeable about the Internet and have a real concern with the problem of having sufficient time to remain current in terms of Internet-using skills.[148] They are concerned that the Internet will cause the need for more professional training.[149]

Studies reveal that librarians have received different forms of Internet training. Some studies report that most librarians receive training from a peer or learn how to use the Internet through self-instruction.[150] Other studies contradict this claim, reporting a majority of librarians attending formal training sessions.[151] In all likelihood, it is probably a mixture of self-instruction and formal training that librarians use to enhance their competencies as Internet users. It is very interesting to note that librarians have been very keen to formulate a role for themselves as Internet trainers, in spite of the fact that data reveal a reluctance among many users to attend formal training classes and a preference for

learning how to use the Internet from a close friend or colleague
or by self-instruction. Studies have reinforced this view and recommended that librarians work with systems professionals to
develop online instructional materials, which allow users to develop Internet skills on their own.[152]

Use of the Internet by University and College Students

The third group of users of the Internet in the academic community is students. Students in many ways overlap with academics
in their using of Internet services. In fact, some studies have included both academics and students in the same sample.[153] The
information behavior of university students is regularly triggered
by information needs imposed by faculty members and course
instructors—the setting of assignments, homework, class activities, and so on. Students also regularly interact with librarians as
they face the various information-related challenges of coursework. These behaviors have been studied to produce general
models of information-seeking behavior.[154] They have also been
studied in order to understand how university students are using
the Internet to support the demands of their learning. These studies use a variety of methods to collect data on student usings of
the Internet, including print-based surveys,[155] electronic questionnaires,[156] focus groups,[157] and various combinations of these
methods.[158]

Frequency of Internet Use

It is not surprising that research reveals college students using the Internet frequently. For this group of users, computing
technologies and the Internet are routine and commonplace. Data
on the frequency of Internet usage by students vary across studies, with somewhere between half[159] and three-quarters[160] of students using the Internet at least once per week. Other studies re-

port a majority of students using the Web between several times a day and several times per week.[161] College students spend about eight hours online every week.[162]

It is, of course, impossible to get a precise fix on the frequency of Internet use by all college students, but research data certainly suggest a continuing rise in the amount of time that students are spending online. College and university students are significant users of the Internet in terms of expertise, proportion, and frequency. For reasons already stated, this is not surprising. The academic and educational sector is a long-term Internet use environment where people find ready access to the equipment and expertise that facilitate use, not to mention a broad range of professional and situational incentives for using the services of the network. In fact, research has revealed that approximately one-third of Internet users obtain access to the Internet through educational providers and slightly more than one-quarter of all users of the Internet are full-time college students.[163]

Gender and Age

The literature on technology adoption and use has speculated about the impact of age and gender upon how an individual will use technology. Internet studies reveal little difference in student frequencies of use and time online across age groups, but there is some evidence that older students are more likely to access the Internet from a home computer, whereas younger students will be more likely to use campus facilities.[164]

Similarly, studies of the impact of gender on frequency of Internet use reveal mixed results. Where one study reveals that male and female college students are online in equal numbers,[165] other studies report a slight majority of female[166] or male usage.[167] The average time online does vary for males and females. Male college students tend to be online twice as long per week as female college students.[168]

When use of particular services is analyzed, the distinction between the usings of male and female college students becomes more apparent. Male students outnumber female students retrieving graphics, downloading software, and using FTP archives for searching.[169] Female students, on the other hand, spend more time using email services than male students.[170]

Internet Services Used

All college students are very active users of email.[171] They are also heavy users of the World Wide Web,[172] using search engines to locate information on the Web.[173] Most use Internet-based library services and discussion groups, but a smaller proportion use Internet relay chat and multiuser dungeons.[174] A majority of college students do not as yet have personal home pages.[175]

Reasons for Internet Use

Studies reveal that college students and faculty go online for different reasons. Faculty use of the Internet is very closely tied to the professional roles that they perform for the university, their discipline, and their professional community. Students also use the Internet for academic purposes such as emailing professors and accessing syllabi and class announcements.[176] College students use the Internet when they are enrolled in a course that is taught via the network. They appreciate the flexibility that this offers in terms of choosing when to study, but characteristically they tend to manage their learning much the same as they would for a course that is not Web-based. For example, most students still print out Web-based course materials before reading them and take no steps toward changing preferred approaches to their learning.[177]

It is very interesting to note that a significant proportion of college students are also using the Internet for nonacademic purposes. Seeking information for nonacademic purposes is almost as commonplace as seeking information for academic purposes.[178] Academic work is still a very important use of the Internet, but students also report using the Internet to maintain relationships with friends and family, to meet new people, to experiment socially, to seek sexual material, and to seek illegal or immoral material. Many students spend more time online for personal reasons than for academic or professional tasks.[179]

Research on Internet use by college students reveals substantial nonacademic usage because these studies have generally been designed to study the broader Internet usings of this group rather than focusing on their professional usings of the Internet (as we saw in the study of academics and librarians). We might speculate that college students have more time to experiment with various usings of the Internet, but it is also likely that studies of professional groups are less likely to reveal nonprofessional usings of the Internet because participants will be less inclined to report using the Internet for personal reasons when the context of the investigation is the workplace.

Use of the Internet by college students for purposes other than academic pursuits is also responsive to gender differences. Female students use the Internet for educational purposes more than male students do, and male students use the Internet for recreation more than female students do.[180] In spite of the fact that females are using the Internet more for educational purposes, male students are citing more Internet resources in the papers they are writing at college. Female students are also using the Internet more than male students for social communication with friends both on the same campus and on other campuses. In fact, making friends and maintaining friendships via the Internet is more common among female students than it is among male students.[181]

Internet Addiction

Widespread use of the Internet by college students has a down side, which has been the focus of several recent studies. These studies have explored the phenomenon of "Internet addiction," based on the view that college students as a group may be more inclined than any other segment of society to develop a form of dependence on the Internet.[182] It is speculated that the reason for this is a combination a factors, including a motivation to develop a strong sense of identity and meaningful and intimate relationships, free and easily accessible connections, and the implicit if not explicit encouragement of Internet use.[183] It is difficult to know just what the impact of Internet addiction might be. Obviously an Internet addict spends so much time online that other activities must suffer. Not surprisingly, Internet addicts report that the Internet has negatively impacted their life routines (work and study), but they also report that the Internet has positively impacted their relationships.[184] It should be stated that the numbers of Internet-dependent students is still very small by proportion to the overall number of student users of the network.

The characteristics of Internet addiction are various, but the most obvious symptom is the amount of time that addicts will spend online. An Internet addict can spend almost three times as many hours online as a nonaddict. They also tend to spend more time on bulletin boards, email, the World Wide Web, and games than students who are not addicted.[185] Addicts also use more Internet sites[186] for a wider variety of reasons than other students.[187] In particular, Internet-dependent students spend more time on the Internet for social reasons than nonaddicted students. It stands to reason that college students are unlikely to become addicted to using the Internet for working on their assignments and coursework commitments, and studies do show that dependent students are more likely to use the Internet for social experimentation and controversial issues such as seeking sexual, illegal, or immoral material than were nonaddicted students.[188] This is confirmed by more-recent studies showing pathological users more likely to use the Internet for meeting new people, using adults-only resources, emotional support, talking to others who share the same interests, playing games, recreation or relaxation, gambling, virtual reality, and wasting time.[189]

Of course, it is impossible to predict Internet addiction, but studies do reveal that it is more likely for a male student to become Internet dependent than it is for a female student.[190] Internet-dependent students also tend to be lonelier.[191] These individuals are often seeking communication experiences. In fact, a recent study explored the assumption that Internet users experience a form of communication pleasure from using the Internet, and the more pleasure they experience, the more they use it.[192] Data from this study confirmed that self-reported communication pleasure experience was the most powerful predictor of Internet addiction among college students.

Internet Instruction

Like their faculty counterparts, college students are unlikely to have learned how to use the Internet through a formal instruction program.[193] The majority of students learn how to use the Internet by surfing (trial and error) and by asking classmates and friends.[194]

Attitudes toward the Internet

Most college students feel that the Internet is playing a positive role in their lives.[195] They think that the Internet is useful[196] and either very important or quite important to their future education.[197] They perceive the network as containing huge amounts of information that will support any point of view that they may be researching.[198]

College student attitudes toward the Internet can vary for males and females. Female students are more likely to feel disoriented on the Internet than their male counterparts. Female students are also more likely to report that they are unable to find their way around the Internet effectively and often get lost, feel that they are not in control, complain that the Internet is too unstructured and too big, view searching the Internet as too difficult and uncertain, claim that using the Internet is not enjoyable, and only use it when they have to. By contrast, male students appear happier to spend time on the Internet, are willing to plough through more irrelevant information in search of relevant information, are more inclined to take courses that are offered entirely via the Internet, and claim that they really enjoy using the Internet.[199] These qualities may suggest that female college students are more discriminating users of the Internet than male

students. Female college students may be less inclined to accept
the shortcomings of the Internet as compensation for using the
technology. In terms of the major themes of this book, it may be
female users who are the most effective agents for user-driven
innovation because this group is less likely (for college students
at least) to accept innovation at face value. Technology must be
an effective tool for reaching a goal. For them, using technology
is not a goal in and of itself.

Cognitive style also plays a role in college student acceptance of some of the qualities of Internet use. College student
searchers who use what researchers call a "searching model" that
is consistent with hypermedia environments are more successful
in searching for information on the Internet than college students
who use a traditional information-retrieval model for their
searching.[200] "Information overload" associated with searching
and the World Wide Web is a problem for college students, but
the graphic orientation of the Web appears to be helping older
college students cope with this. College students who are verbal-
izers by cognitive style are also more likely to suffer from information overload and anxieties that may be associated with
using the Internet.[201]

College student attitudes toward the Internet as an information source for coursework have been studied and compared to
the way college students view traditional information sources
such as the university library. College students tend to choose
between these sources according to the assignment due date (the
sooner the deadline, the more likely a student will use the Internet), the nature of the topic (e.g., humanities—library; current
information on science and technology—Internet), and the directions received from the course instructor.[202] It is interesting to
note that college students don't see the Internet as a library resource and rarely consider asking a librarian for assistance with
locating information on the Internet.[203] They have real difficulty
distinguishing between commercial library resources delivered
over the Internet and Internet information resources.[204]

Having chosen to search for information on the Internet, college students report moderate levels of satisfaction with both the

process and the results of their information seeking. Characteristically, college students will search the Internet using a search engine and may have a particular, favored search engine that they use repeatedly. The problems that college students report when searching the Internet include: they don't find the information they need; there is no full-text information; or their searching results in too many hits.[205] The majority of college students see the Internet as a resource for finding current academic information,[206] but do not necessarily identify the network or the Web as their first choice for finding the information that they need for their studies.[207] With experience, college students quickly become sophisticated in being able to determine when the Internet is the most useful and appropriate research tool for a particular task.[208] They can generally evaluate the quality of an Internet site and the reliability of the information that they locate on that site in relation to the academic task at hand.[209]

Use of the Internet by Teachers

As the Internet has developed, the rhetoric associated with educational benefits derived from access to the resources of the network has gathered sufficient momentum to bring about a widespread acceptance of the importance of access to the Internet by all stakeholders in the educational community. In preceding sections of this chapter, we have discussed members of the college and university community (faculty, students and academic librarians). Clearly, the school community has also been affected by widespread use of the Internet. Internet terminals are available in schools and increasingly in classrooms, and some teachers are incorporating the Internet into their curriculum.

Most of the key stakeholders in Internet development have an interest in how teachers are using the Internet because schools are providing technology socialization for the next generation of Internet users. Use of the Internet by teachers has therefore been the subject of numerous studies that have applied various methods of data collection such as paper-based questionnaires,[210]

Web-based surveys,[211] qualitative interviews,[212] and a method called the Fast Response Survey System (commissioned by the National Center for Education Statistics).[213]

Internet Access

Studies of teachers using the Internet often determine a teacher's access to the network based on data related to school access. Studies will claim, for example, that almost all teachers have access to the Internet in the school building.[214] In the United States, over 90 percent of schools have some sort of access to the Internet someplace in the school building,[215] and almost all full-time teachers have access to the Internet somewhere in their schools.[216] The assumption that teachers have access to the Internet because the school is connected to the network can be misleading, however, because studies also reveal that up to two-thirds of teachers do not know where the computers with Internet access are located in their schools.[217] Approximately one-half of teachers in the United States have some kind of Internet access in their own classroom,[218] and access to the Internet in the classroom is about as common for teachers as having access to the Internet in their homes. In fact, studies show that most teachers who use the Internet for professional reasons are connecting to the network from home rather than from school.[219] A little more than half of the teachers in several recent studies report that they have some form of Internet access in their own homes, but a moderate proportion of teachers have *no* access to the Internet, either at home or in the classroom.[220]

Internet Use

Given the extent of the access that the teaching profession has to computers with Internet access, it is not surprising that studies reveal large proportions of teachers using the Internet for professional purposes such as researching and planning lessons.[221] In some studies, all the teacher participants describe themselves as Internet users[222] even when their frequency of

Internet use is as low as once per week.[223] In fact, teachers are generally not high-frequency users of the Internet. Frequencies of use are increasing, but the majority of teachers appear to be accessing and using the Internet only about once or twice a week[224] or about five and a half hours per month.[225] Frequency of Internet use can also vary depending on the discipline taught. Social studies teachers, for example, are lower-frequency users of the network.[226]

Like a number of other professional groups appearing in this book, teachers are motivated to use the Internet by a number of factors. Teachers report a curiosity and a desire to learn more about the Internet particularly in relation to their professional roles, but research is also revealing that teachers feel some pressure to use the Internet because of job demands and student interest as well as pressure from the school administration and the educational hyperbole presented in the media.[227] Teachers are using the Internet for professional activities[228] such as creating instructional materials[229] and finding information resources that they can use in their lessons. Most teachers are not integrating Internet use into their classroom activities, however.[230] For many, the Internet is a professional resource or tool but not a key component of the learning environment.[231]

It is also interesting to note that, in general, only a small proportion of teachers are using email to communicate with fellow teachers. Early studies showed email as the most commonly used Internet service by teachers,[232] but more recent research reveals that uses of email such as communicating with other teachers, other classes, or other Internet users is rare.[233] It is also uncommon for teachers to engage in interactive aspects of Internet use[234] such as posting information, suggestions, opinions, or student work on the World Wide Web.[235]

There are several demographic factors that may predict whether or not a teacher uses the Internet. Using of the Internet can vary according to a teacher's age, for example; younger teachers are more likely to use the Internet professionally and to consider the Internet essential to their classroom environment.[236] Newer teachers (in terms of how long a person has been teaching) are a little more likely to use the Internet to accomplish various teaching objectives,[237] but generally the relationship between Internet use and years of teaching experience is weak.[238] Interestingly, the college that a teacher attended has a significant effect on predicting how a teacher will use the Internet with his or her students. Even the teacher's own success in school makes a difference when it comes to predicting Internet use. Teachers with higher grade point averages are more inclined toward using the Internet in their teaching.[239] There is no difference between levels of schooling, however—between the Internet uses of teachers with a master's degree as opposed to teachers with a bachelor's degree.[240]

It is unclear if gender has any effect on the way a teacher uses the Internet. Some studies have found that there is no difference in the way male and female teachers use the Internet,[241] but there does appear to be a difference in how frequently male and female teachers use the network. Male teachers are more likely to be regular users of the Internet than are female teachers.[242]

Not surprisingly, classroom connectivity is a strong predictor of Internet use by teachers.[243] Teachers who have access to the Internet in their classrooms are far more likely to be regular users of the network. Continued and regular use of the Internet by teachers is also related to their access to technological resources generally.[244] Both home and classroom access to technology are equally related to Internet use. Teachers who have a combination of home and classroom access tend to be more frequent users of the Internet.[245] Level of access to technology and the frequency of Internet use obviously play a role in predicting teacher expertise and this in turn will affect how a teacher perceives the Internet in relation to their work. Generally, teachers who are more expert with technology and the Internet are more likely to value the Internet as an essential part of the teaching and learning process.[246] Expertise is, of course, related to training. Teachers who have received training tend to be more inclined to regard the Internet as an essential classroom resource.[247]

Perceptions of the Internet as an essential classroom resource and its integration into teaching practice are likely to be related to a teacher's pedagogy and teaching philosophy. Teachers who are constructivist, as opposed to traditional, in their pedagogies have a more positive view of the Internet.[248] In particular, the pedagogies of nonacademic-core teachers (most often in business and other occupation-related fields) appear to be most affected by higher levels of Internet use in the classroom.[249] Some teachers are also innovators and early adopters of technology. Teachers who have had their students use computer software in a substantial way for several years or who have been among the pioneer teachers employing Internet-based activities for classes of students tend to be the same teachers who are most likely to report that teaching practice has changed substantially over the past years in ways that educational theorists would characterize as a constructivist-oriented model of teaching.[250] These teachers are innovative by nature and, as such, are more likely to use network technologies in teaching and learning.[251] Teachers who are leaders are also more likely to use the Internet with their students and in their own professional activities.[252] A positive attitude toward the Internet is the key to perceiving the network as an essential classroom resource. Teachers who are excited about using the Internet tend to become regular users of the network.[253] Indeed, a teacher's use of the Internet is dependent on his or her attitude toward using the network as an instructional tool and willingness to restructure classes and to rethink approaches to teaching.[254]

Initial acceptance and use of the Internet by teachers is, of course, varied and can be a function of factors such as the perceived relevance of Internet resources, teacher workload and schedule, or the amount of success that a teacher has had during initial encounters with the network.[255] Internet use by teachers is predicted by a complex set of personal and professional values. Teachers who are creative users of the Internet will often discuss subjects about which they lack expertise and allow themselves to be taught by students, orchestrate multiple simultaneous activities during class time, assign long and complex projects for students to undertake, and give students greater choice in their tasks and the materials and resources they can use to complete them.[256]

The degree to which a teacher has a positive attitude toward the Internet or values the Internet as an instructional resource can vary according to the subject taught. Computer teachers have the most positive attitude toward the Internet and use the network more than other teachers for student research and student projects. Science and English teachers also have slightly higher value perceptions of the Internet,[257] and science teachers use the Internet more than teachers of the humanities.[258] Mathematics teachers appear to value the Internet the least[259] and use it less in classroom teaching than do teachers in other subject areas.[260]

Grade level taught also influences the extent to which a teacher will use the Internet. High school teachers use the Internet more frequently than middle school teachers and middle school teachers use the network more frequently than elementary school teachers.[261] In a similar way, the abilities of the students taught can have an influence on the extent to which a teacher will use the Internet. Teachers who work with high-achieving students are more likely to use the Internet and regard it as an essential teaching tool than teachers assigned to normal stream classes. Teachers of "average" classes are in turn slightly more likely to use the Internet for teaching purposes than teachers assigned to classes in lower streams.[262]

The level of poverty of the school district and community has an obvious impact on Internet use. Teachers who are working in schools with lower school-poverty levels are more likely to use the Internet for creating instructional materials than teachers in schools with high poverty levels.[263] The major barriers to Internet use by teachers are not necessarily financial, however. The most common barriers to using the Internet are a lack of training for teachers, particularly in how to apply Internet resources and services to classroom instruction and technical problems related to Internet access within the classroom.[264] The general lack of technical support in the school environment is a major hurdle for teachers.[265] Teachers complain that they do not have the time to learn how to use and effectively apply new technologies such as the Internet and that they are constantly confronting the skepticism of administrators[266] who are concerned about students accessing inappropriate materials.

It is difficult to determine how prepared teachers feel in relation to using the Internet in their classrooms. While the most common complaint from teachers is that they don't have time to learn how to use the Internet well, a majority also claim that they feel comfortable using the Internet in their classrooms.[267] Teachers with fewer years of experience and those who have had more hours of professional development tend to feel better prepared,[268] but like other professional groups described in this book, teachers tend to learn how to use the Internet on their own (self-instruction) or turn to colleagues for assistance.[269] Few teachers have attended formal courses or workshops on how to use the Internet.[270] Most prefer to learn about the Internet in the context of their daily work where they can apply techniques and tools to classroom instruction or administration.[271]

In spite of the concerns and barriers that can prevent effective using of the Internet, teachers are generally enthusiastic about the network.[272] They are positive about the resources that they can access via the Internet and see these as definitely useful in the classroom.[273] For these reasons, most teachers would like to be using the Internet more than they currently are[274] and consider access to the network in their classrooms, particularly a teacher's workstation with email access, as essential.[275]

Child and Young Adult Internet Users

The group of users who will have the greatest impact on the future development of the Internet are the child and young adult users of the network. This group of users is growing up with the Internet. They do not know of a world *without* internetworked information services, have never searched a card catalog, and regard browsing websites and using Web search engines as commonplace. They are members of the digital generation or net generation. They are the immediate and long-term beneficiaries of networked educational initiatives, e-democracy, Internet commerce, and a host of network services as yet unknown. They are a market for future Internet services and resources and their usings of the Internet today will fashion the developments of the Internet in the future.

Researchers have used various methods of data collection to gain insight into the Internet behaviors of young users including questionnaires,[276] data logs and content analysis,[277] field research[278] or a combination of several approaches.[279]

Internet Access

One of the features of children and young adults using the Internet is that this group of users is increasingly exposed to the Internet in the home. It is no surprise that studies are revealing a high proportion of youths and teens living in homes that have a computer.[280] This does not necessarily mean that the home also has Internet access, but nearly three-quarters of young people in the United States, for example, live in homes with access to the network. Internet access in the home is directly related to household income.[281] Young people living in high-income, highly educated families are much more likely to have access to the Internet from their family home.[282]

Internet Use

Living in a home with Internet access does not necessarily mean that a young person will use the Internet, however. Numerous studies of young people simply assume that members of this group are Internet users because they are exposed to the network in their schools and have access to an Internet-enabled computer in their home. Many such studies do not ask directly if participants in the study sample are Internet users or not. The proportion of young people actually using the Internet on a regular basis is, therefore, unclear. What is clear is that almost all young people have used the Internet at some time or another, but a smaller proportion are advancing to using the Internet in a self-sufficient way and thereby identify themselves as Internet users.[283]

Related to how many young people are using the Internet is the frequency of this use. How frequently does a young, regular user of the Internet access the services of the network? Studies of teenagers in Kuala Lumpur,[284] Israel,[285] and the United States[286] report that teenagers are using the Internet on average about five hours per week. Male teenagers tend to use the Internet more frequently than female teenagers.[287] In fact, race, gender, and generation are all fairly strong predictors of Internet use. White, teenage males, for example, use the Internet more frequently than adult, female minorities.[288] The frequency of Internet use also decreases with the age of children. Younger children spend less time and use the Internet less frequently than older children.[289]

Most teenagers rate themselves as highly skilled users of the Internet,[290] but they are generally reluctant to share this expertise with their parents and families.[291] If a child happens to be the heaviest user of the Internet in a family, however, the average use by other family members does tend to increase by their example. The enthusiasm of a family member will motivate other family members to use the Internet, and those with skill will help other family members to overcome barriers.[292]

Most young people are learning how to use the network in an educational context. Much of what we know about young people using the Internet has been gleaned from studies of Internet use in the classroom and in school libraries. The data on Internet use by young people reveal that almost all students are using the Internet at school, where they are shown how to use network services as learning tools. In light of this, it is surprising that, like other groups already treated in this chapter (e.g., academics), young people, particularly teenagers, are inclined to teach themselves how to use the Internet rather than relying on their teachers to show them how to use the network.[293] Young people also learn how to use the Internet from their friends.[294] For younger children, initial instruction on how to use the Internet is often provided at home by the mother.[295]

A significant proportion of young people, in fact, prefer to use the Internet at home[296] because here they are more likely to use the network for fun and to make friends.[297] Young people frequently use the Internet for surfing and browsing,[298] and while they generally prefer to surf the Internet on their own, many young people also surf the Web with friends.[299]

Reasons for Internet Use

Young people use the Internet to communicate with their friends and peers. Affiliation and affirmation are strong drivers in the behavior of young people. The primary focus of Internet use is communication (e.g., email, chat), but studies reveal that parental concerns about who young people might be communicating with over the Internet is distorting the data that we have on this type of Internet use.[300] Parentally imposed limits on computer access in the home may be artificially lowering the levels of Internet use for communication by young people.[301] We therefore find that young children use the Internet for communication but not as intensively as teenagers.[302]

Parents are also concerned about young people accessing offensive materials when browsing the World Wide Web. It is interesting to note that studies focusing on this issue reveal that young people are making very little contact with this sort of material via the Internet[303] and that there is little evidence that material being accessed is having effects on children that would concern parents or caregivers.[304]

One of the most popular uses of the Internet by young people is to play games and to find game-cheating sites. One recent study found that more than one-third of the sites visited by the young people in the sample were sites where games could be played.[305] Sites where young people can learn the solutions to games (game-cheating sites) are also very popular.[306] Boys tend to be far more enthusiastic than girls about using the Internet to download games.[307]

As mentioned previously, young people are using the Internet extensively in schools. They are learning how to use the services of the network to support their learning. They are learning information-searching skills and becoming information and technology literate. Young people, therefore, use the Internet for study-related purposes.[308] They search for images they can download for school assignments. They locate and verify facts and print off information found on websites.[309] They use the Internet to do their homework and to find out about news and current events and health education.[310]

Studies show that there are gender differences when it comes to locating information for schoolwork. Girls are more motivated than boys to find information on education-related topics.[311] Female pairs of students working together to complete an educational task on the Internet are also far more collaborative in this endeavor than their male counterparts. They complete Internet tasks more efficiently and make fewer mistakes.[312]

Young people like to use the Internet to locate information. In fact, the Internet ranks third after peers and parents as the preferred information source.[313] Young people are impressed by the different types of information that they can locate on the World Wide Web. They like being able to access pictures and they think that information on the Internet is easy to locate and is up to date.[314] On the whole, the Internet is considered a fast and efficient information tool.[315]

Attitudes toward the Internet

Teenagers can also be frustrated when they use the Internet. They become frustrated with the network when they cannot open a site, misspell search terms, or have difficulty remembering or typing a URL correctly or when response times are too long or a search becomes time consuming.[316] Some of this frustration arises from unrealistic expectations. The majority of young people believe that all the information they locate on the Internet is reliable and valid.[317] In fact, young people believe that their grades will be somehow better because they have used the World Wide Web to do their work[318] and can therefore be surprised when teachers do not reinforce this expectation with a high grade.

In spite of the obvious opportunities for frustration with Internet searching, young people are, in fact, rarely dissatisfied[319] with their Internet searches, even when the search is clearly not successful in terms of locating the information they need.[320] It has been suggested that this can be explained by the fact that young people have a different way of determining what is relevant.[321] There is certainly evidence to suggest that young people engage in very little planning when they are approaching an information-seeking task.[322] They have difficulty describing their search strategy and in fact perform better on an ill-defined information task than on a well-defined one.[323] This may be because the well-defined task requires analytic search strategies and the ill-defined task can often be solved by browsing the Web. In fact, the search strategy of choice for young people is browsing the World Wide Web.[324]

E-Government Information Internet Users

Many of the Internet developments described in previous sections of this book have arisen from federal government initiatives based on assumptions that the general public will benefit from access to the Internet. The notions of an information infrastructure and later a global information infrastructure, for example, were promoted by the rhetoric that social, cultural, and political equities will arise from a wired and connected community. It makes sense that government departments and utilities were among the first agencies to begin publishing and disseminating information via the Internet and today this is a widespread practice. The United States government, for example, is the largest information provider in the world, producing multimillions of publications annually. The federal government has been posting websites since 1993 and subsequent incentives such as the Paperwork Reduction Act of 1995 mean that today many government information services are accessible via the World Wide

Web. A recent study identified nearly 900 federal websites and many of these sites were being extensively used.[325] It was found, for example, that users were downloading an average of 2.5 million documents per month from over seventy databases on the Government Printing Office Access Website. Unfortunately, in spite of this incredible growth in the number of government sites, very little attention has be paid to standards, the searching abilities of users, or the way this information is being accessed and used.

The publication and dissemination of government information via the Internet is supported by a widely accepted, "myth-like" narrative which presents us with a set of assumptions about information and its role in civil life. This information democracy narrative claims:

1. That access to "good information" is critical for the working of "good democracy";
2. That when information is allowed to flow freely in a free marketplace, "truth" or "the best information" naturally surfaces much like cream in fresh whole milk;
3. That the value of "good information" is such that any rational person will seek it out and that therefore, availability equals accessibility;
4. That "good information" ought to be available to all citizens in a democracy, that there should be no information inequities; and
5. That it is unfortunate that some citizens have fewer resources, and that we must therefore provide means of access to "good information" for these citizens.[326]

Acceptance of these assumptions has underpinned the development of most government information sites and services. In the simplest form, these sites and services are a Web presence for standard departmental information publishing. In other words, government departments are publishing print-based public documents on the World Wide Web. Clearly, this simple translation is based on the assumption that making these documents available through the Internet increases the likelihood that people (citizens) will make contact with the information that govern-

ment departments are promoting. In fact, there is some evidence
to suggest that simply building the information site will be
enough to attract a small base of users to the government information stored there.[327] Whatever benefits incidentally arise from
people being exposed to this information are implied and assumed. Most government departments are at this stage in their
development of an Internet presence.

The next stage in the development of an e-government Internet presence is to provide the tools for two-way communication
and information exchange. In this case, citizens not only have
access to government information but also have access to the
services of a government department. This will mean access to
the experts, opinions, interpretations, and advice that a government department normally provides through its physical presence. It may also involve an extension of conventional service.
From stage one, where a government department mounts its information on the Web, the using of this information will evolve
this resource into a service.

Once people have access to information in a two-way environment, it is a natural inclination to pursue alternative forms of
this information. For example, questions are posed about the information. People begin to request the information in different
forms or formats. People want parts of the information entity
rather than the complete package. Others want related information or may want to publish their own information on the site. If
the e-government site is responsive to these forms of interaction,
then quantifiable exchanges of value to people begin to take
place. For example, citizens may be able to pay a fine or renew a
license rather than simply accessing information about the location of a department and its office hours. Some sites like this are
appearing on the Internet at the state and local government levels.

The final stage in the evolution of e-government is where we
see the development of a portal that integrates the complete
range of government services. These services are provided via
the Internet and arranged by need and function, not on the basis
of bureaucratic or departmental preferences. Many governments

have made plans to develop their e-government presence in this way. There are still very few examples (e.g., MAXI, operated by the state of Victoria in Australia and the eCitizen Centre in Singapore)[328] of this form of e-government site, however, and it is unclear how they will be used and how satisfied people will be with this form of service. A recent study of people using an Internet-based facility for filing tax returns in Taiwan, for example, found that levels of user satisfaction for people using this sort of service were generally low.[329]

E-government is also associated with e-democracy. Manifestations of democratic behavior on the Internet come in the forms of political activity using the Internet and also e-voting. Most political parties and affiliations have a Web presence and promote their views using Web or Internet technologies. For example, around 5 to 6 percent of people participating in a study during the 1996 election season in the United States indicated that they were contacted by candidate organizations and national political organizations via email.[330] People who use the websites of political parties and candidates for office also indicate that these sites facilitate their participation in the democratic process and improve the observability of public office holders.[331] This appears true for Europe as well as the United States. A recent large-scale survey involving citizens of European Union member countries found that, for people using e-government sites on the Internet, more than one-third were interested in using the Internet to participate in political debates.[332]

Voting on the Internet is possible, but in the United States the Federal Election Commission has not yet approved it. There is some concern that the public does not have sufficient confidence in an election process conducted over the Internet, and there is caution about moving too quickly in this direction. Forrester Research is predicting that Internet voting will not occur in the United States for at least two or more presidential elections.[333]

Use of Government Information Online

Who are the people using these services and accessing this information and what are their perceptions of e-government and government information on the Internet? Unfortunately, there have been very few studies that focus on the users of government information on the Internet. The studies that do exist provide a description of users and usings of electronic government information based on data collected by questionnaires,[334] telephone interviews,[335] content analysis of email messages,[336] experiments and follow-up survey questionnaire,[337] and telephone and Web-based surveys.[338]

People who use government information are choosing to access this information via the Internet in preference to printed formats. Users of government document libraries, for example, choose to access the information they need from Internet sites using terminals in the library,[339] and reference work in government document libraries is increasingly based upon online material. People who use government information are also accessing this information on the Internet frequently. Small business executives, for example, are frequent users of government information on the Internet,[340] and people who use networked information services that are provided by legislative representatives are not describing themselves as casual users.[341]

Types of Information Accessed

It is difficult to determine the types of government information being accessed using the Internet, but federal government sites are generally accessed more regularly than state sites and regulatory and legislative types of information are considered the most important.[342] Generally, users of government information on the Internet value most highly the information they could not have accessed by other means.[343] This information is generally not used for job-related purposes. For example, a recent study that examined the content of email requests to a government aging service revealed that most requests were made for information about caring for a family member.[344]

Factors Affecting Use of Government Information

There is some evidence that being aware that government information is available on the Internet is related to the likelihood that a person will search for this information.[345] If a person knows that a site is available, he or she is more likely to search for information on that site. Levels of awareness of the content and format of government information on the Internet are generally low, however. Awareness may be relative to age. Younger small business executives, for example, are more likely to search for the government information they need on the Internet than older small business executives; they also tend to visit more government information sites.[346]

Women are more likely than men to use government information on the Internet. This may correspond with the types of government information available and the possible uses of this information. Family information, for example, is more likely to be accessed and used by females than males. Interestingly, women tend to access this information in an indirect way. A recent study found that nearly one-third of the requests to e-government sites that were initiated by females did not come from their own email account. These data indicate that the prospect of making contact with an agency in this manner is important enough, for women at least, to gain access to email though a friend, family member, or public access point (such as a library).[347]

E-Commerce Internet Users

There is little doubt that market forces played a major role in the development of the Internet through the 1990s. As a broad-based public access agenda took hold and more and more people began using the Internet, it was clear to commercial interests that the network presented a unique opportunity to access markets of a scale well beyond the reach of many small and even large businesses. The behavior, attitudes, beliefs, and attributes of a new form of Internet user (the e-commerce user or online consumer) have therefore been the focus of a great deal of research activity. This research has spanned a number of fields, including marketing, information science, business, and human-computer interaction.

The behaviors associated with this form of Internet use are consuming or purchasing behaviors as opposed to information or communication behaviors, though there is a great deal of overlap. These are very instrumental usings of the Internet which are in many ways associated with a changing perception of normal human activities such as communicating with the family, writing, listening, managing money and financial commitments, and shopping for some goods and services.[348] Many businesses are selling products online such as books, groceries, music, and so on. Other businesses are selling services (communication or information) such as stock information. A lot has been written about the types of organizations that transition more readily to a networked environment. Indeed, some observers are noting that commercial enterprise on a global scale, based on a powerful information infrastructure, is transforming the orientation, structure, and physical organization of many businesses. Companies are shifting from a product- or manufacturing-centered orientation to a service- or knowledge-centered orientation.[349]

Some of what we know about online consumers has been obtained by online profiling. Techniques for online profiling were developed in the mid- to late 1990s when the potential for advertising contact with the growing number of Internet users first became apparent. The scope and scale of this activity is enormous. A recent report on online profiling, for example, states that Internet advertising revenues in the United States alone grew from $301 million in 1996 to $4.62 billion in 1999.[350] These revenues are projected to reach $11.5 billion in 2003.

The profiling of people using the Web is accomplished by the use of "cookies" and "web bugs" which track a person's actions on the network. The sorts of data gathered include information about the websites a consumer has visited, the search terms that an individual used, and the pathways that led a consumer to the page monitored by the advertising network developing the online profile. In spite of the fact that network advertisers and their profiling activities have become almost ubiquitous, consumers are generally unaware that their Internet activities are being monitored. Once the detailed information about an individual is analyzed and combined with data about the consumer's online purchases or data that a consumer may have provided through online surveys or registrations, the advertising functions of online profiling kick in. The detailed profile facilitates predictions of consumer behavior, tastes, and purchasing habits and delivers advertisements to the consumer's desktop that are directly targeted at the interests of the individual.

It is important to note that the studies reviewed for this description of online consumers did not use online profiling. This research collected data using a variety of other methods such as online survey questionnaires[351] distributed by email,[352] the web,[353] or telephone;[354] focus group interviews;[355] open-ended interviews;[356] and controlled experiments.[357]

How Popular Is Online Buying?

In spite of the incredible growth in online commercial activity, the proportion of people who are otherwise users of the Internet and who are using the network to make purchases online is still small. We are, of course, still talking about large numbers of people, because the overall number of users of the Internet is growing at an exponential rate. The proportion of Internet users who are shopping online varies in studies from as low as 15 percent to as high as 57 percent. These data are generally based upon asking participants to report if they have ever made a purchase online. A recent study of Internet users in Singapore, for example, found that over 25 percent of the people surveyed had made an Internet purchase.[358] Other studies report that 42 percent,[359] 54 percent,[360] or as few as 16 percent[361] of participants had at some time purchased goods online. The amount of money that people are spending on the Internet also varies, but the average transaction is valued at around $30 and this is true for the United States, Asia, and Europe.[362]

What Are Consumers Buying?

The question of what people are buying on the Internet and indeed what people would be willing to purchase over the Internet is critical. If we accept that the development of the network is following a using trajectory and market forces are catalyzing this process, then buying and consuming patterns will fundamentally influence the future development of Internet interfaces and technologies. Studies show that Internet users are more likely to purchase intangible or informational goods such as online financial information or computer software than they are to purchase tangible or physical goods such as jewelry or cars. Products with high differentiation are also more suited for sale on the Internet than are products with low differentiation like eggs and milk. Online shoppers, particularly female shoppers, are very wary of purchasing items that require proper fit and texture.[363] Software, books, and magazines account for over half of the online purchases made by women.[364] Online shoppers generally are purchasing videos and music, subscriptions to financial reports and stock market quotes, computer software and computer games, videos, exercise equipment, and bicycles.[365]

Attitudes toward Online Buying

Not surprisingly, there is a range of reasons that people give for buying goods and services online. For some, it is the attractiveness of the offer. Others focus on qualities of the transaction such as a fast response time or the availability of a wider range of products.[366] Females in particular have been rather ambivalent about the online shopping experience. Female shoppers indicate that they are satisfied with the purchases they make but that the overall experience of online shopping is sometimes less than sat-

isfactory. In some cases this relates to a perception on the part of
the shopper that they will be getting more from this experience
than from conventional shopping behaviors. Some women, for
example, declare that there is little difference between the quality
of goods found in their local store and the goods sold on the
Internet.[367] This suggests that these shoppers are looking for
something more than a commercial transaction. If they are to
lose some of the social reinforcements that come from conventional shopping, then they expect to be compensated by some
other value such as enhanced quality of the product or service
purchased.

Factors Predicting Use of the Internet for Online Shopping

Age is one factor that predicts use of the Internet for online
shopping. While we may assume that younger, and therefore
more technology savvy, users of the Internet are more likely to
use the network in this way, this is not the case. Studies are
showing that younger Internet users are looking for entertainment and fun on the Internet, while older users are more likely to
make purchases online. Internet shoppers are older than non-
Internet shoppers,[368] although this can vary depending on the
type of product or service being purchased. People who purchase
travel information on the Internet, for example, are in the middle
age ranges.[369]

There are many other variables that influence purchasing
behaviors on the Internet. Income level is related to online shopping behavior. It has a direct relationship with the number of
hours that a user will spend per day on the Web, the frequency of
Web purchases, the percentage of business Web use, and the
likelihood of a recent Web transaction.[370] In short, Internet shoppers tend to make more money than non-Internet shoppers.[371]
The research findings are mixed concerning the effects of gender
and education as predictors of Internet shopping. One recent
study found that males are slightly more inclined to make Web
purchases;[372] other studies have found no real difference in terms

of the volume or frequency of Internet shopping due to gender.[373]
Males and females do shop differently, of course, and these distinctions in terms of product and quality preferences are true for
Internet and non-Internet shopping. In terms of education, at the
general product level there appears to be no relationship between
education and the likelihood of using the Internet for shopping,[374] but people with college degrees are more likely to search
for travel information or purchase travel products than people at
other education levels.[375] The same is true for people with higher
occupational status.

It stands to reason that the more time a person spends on the
Internet, the more likely it is that he or she will purchase products online. Higher levels of Internet use tend to lead to the using
the Internet for shopping purposes.[376] This may arise because of
the greater likelihood that targeted advertising will reach the
heavier user through the devices of online profiling. Whatever
the reason, studies agree that Internet shoppers are people who
are spending longer amounts of time surfing the World Wide
Web[377] or working online.[378] The heavier users of the Internet are
also more likely to find gratification from features of online
shopping such as convenience and competitive pricing.[379]

In earlier discussion in this book, the attribute of personal
innovativeness was described as a likely predictor of Internet
using. The assumption is that people who are innovative will
tend to adopt a technology and adapt it to various new and perhaps different uses. There is a distinction between general innovativeness and domain-specific innovativeness. Domain-specific
innovativeness is the tendency that an individual may have toward learning about and adopting an innovation within a specific
domain of interest, thereby exploring more deeply the potential
that the innovation might have for transforming that area of interest. Studies of Internet shoppers are finding that where a person has the qualities of domain-specific innovativeness, he or she
is more likely to use the Internet for online shopping or general
business transactions.[380]

Studies of online shopping have indicated that this personality attribute can be a predictor of online shopping behavior for

people using the Internet. Internet shoppers are innovative Internet users (often arising from heavier, domain-specific use) who are more inclined to seek convenience and take risks.[381] Online consumers are people who enjoy the social escapism of the Internet.[382] They are more impulsive and want more variety of product line than might be available via conventional shopping contexts. Online consumers tend to be less brand conscious and price conscious than non-Internet shoppers. They have a more positive attitude toward advertising, but not necessarily a more positive attitude toward shopping in general, than non-Internet shoppers.[383]

Online consumers tend be living a wired lifestyle. As previously described, such people have generally been using the Internet for years and claim that the Internet and communications technology generally have increased their productivity. Time may be an important factor, as well. Many Internet shoppers claim to have limited time for shopping.[384]

Consumer Concerns about E-Commerce

People tend to be concerned about the privacy and security issues associated with online commercial transactions. Internet users are uncertain about the trustworthiness and credibility of online retailers.[385] The top concerns for online consumers are the security of the electronic payment systems and the systems for preventing unauthorized access to Internet shopping sites.[386] In spite of the extraordinary growth of online shopping and e-commerce, Internet users are still cautious when it comes to making a transaction that will require disclosure of credit card numbers. Generally speaking, Internet users have an unfavorable perception of Internet shopping security,[387] and a majority of Internet users are skeptical that a resolution to the issues of security, privacy, and payments will be found in the near future.[388] The biggest concerns that people have with doing business via the Internet are communications security, use of personal information by the vendor, vendor authentication and credibility, and vulnerability of the vendor's network to unauthorized access.[389]

These perceptions are an important concern for the future of online commerce. They clearly must be addressed, but in the meantime it is interesting to note that the identification of these issues is not really stopping Internet users from adopting online commerce. Studies are revealing, for example, that people are willing to provide demographic information online. What they find particularly objectionable is the loss or the transfer of their personal information without their knowledge.[390] The practice of online profiling, discussed earlier, is a version of this. But even when online shoppers are aware that their privacy is being violated in this way, studies indicate this does not necessarily deter the Internet user from shopping online.[391] People continue to purchase online in spite of their concerns.[392] In fact, it has been shown that heavier business users of the Web tend to be less worried about the nontransactional privacy issues.[393] This explains why some people continue to shop online, but for reluctant shoppers or for people who have not yet tried online shopping, the issues of privacy and insecure payment systems are discouraging or preventing them from trying these services.[394]

General Public Users of the Internet

One of the central themes of this book has been the acceptance and use of the Internet by the general public. What began as a middle-up infrastructure, available to an elite band of researchers, scholars, administrators, and public servants is now as commonplace as the telephone and as popular as television.

There have been several large-scale studies of general public users of the Internet. Many of these studies focus on Internet use in specific countries,[395] but there have also been some international Internet surveys conducted.[396] These studies of Internet users and usings apply a variety of methods to collect data, from survey questionnaires based on the Web[397] or distributed electronically[398] to examinations of existing data sets,[399] interviews,[400] written questionnaires,[401] data logs,[402] online surveys, and focus groups.[403]

Internet Use

The statistics that describe Internet use are staggering. It is problematic to quote these because the numbers are increasing so rapidly. For example, in 1996, 25-30 percent of Americans were connected to the Internet, but by the close of the century this figure had doubled.[404] At the beginning of the twenty-first century, 104 million American adults were online; nearly three-quarters of American children between twelve and seventeen years of age had Internet access and over a quarter of American children under twelve years of age had been online.[405]

Age is a strong predictor of Internet use by the general public, and this appears to be the case internationally. Studies of Internet use in the United States,[406] Singapore,[407] Canada,[408] Mexico,[409] and the United Kingdom[410] indicate a positive relationship between age and Internet use.

Early studies of the general public had reported gender as a predictor of Internet use.[411] Individuals who reported not being aware of the Internet were more likely to be female and long-time Internet users of the network were more likely to be male.[412] Although this trend has continued for some cultures, for example, Mexico,[413] recent studies in the United States and the United Kingdom are showing that the gender gap in Internet use is closing. In fact, women are using the Internet slightly more than men in the United States[414] and the proportions for male and female use of the Internet are now almost identical in the United Kingdom.[415]

Internet users come from a wide range of occupations. The largest category of Internet users report themselves as trained professionals working in the private sector.[416] A large proportion of Internet users are students from kindergarten to university.[417] Less well-educated individuals are likely to be less aware of the Internet.[418] In fact, educational level is highly predictive of Internet use. As educational level increases from high school or less to bachelor's degree or higher, the amount of Internet use also increases. It is estimated that more than three-quarters of people with a college degree are using the Internet, whereas only

slightly more than one-third of people with a high school di-
ploma or less are using the services of the network.[419]

There is evidence to suggest that this relationship is contaminated by the association between education and socioeconomic status. One recent study where subjects were provided
with a computer and Internet access revealed that, when economic barriers are removed, people across socioeconomic and
educational lines use the Internet.[420] In fact, numerous studies
have shown that income is predictive of Internet use. As income
increases so does Internet use.[421] Individuals who report that they
are not using the Internet characteristically have lower incomes
and long-time users of the Internet have higher incomes.[422] This
is not to say, of course, that Internet using is a behavior exclusive
to well-off members of the population.[423]

In the same way, race has been found to predict Internet use.
A number of studies are revealing that Internet users are predominantly white.[424] It should be noted, however, that African-
Americans are increasingly likely to find uses for the Internet on
a typical day and the gap between black and white users in terms
of daily Internet use is shrinking.[425]

Generally, people have their first Internet experiences at
work or have friends or family teach them how to use the network.[426] School also plays a critical role for many.[427] People begin using and continue to use the Internet because use of the
network is required for their job or for study. Curiosity about the
Internet is also a key motivating factor.[428] Most commonly, people want to use the Internet to keep in contact with people they
know using email, to acquire information, and to keep themselves up to date.[429] Generally the first Internet service that people use is email, which then draws them to discover other aspects
of the Internet such as the World Wide Web.[430] Email is also
considered the service that keeps people interested in using the
Internet. Email use is self-reinforcing and very stable. When we
examine a person's email use for a particular week, we can characteristically use this data to predict the following week's usage.[431] In fact, for a significant proportion of people, email is the
main or sole reason for using the Internet.[432] Other popular Inter-

net services include the World Wide Web, file transfer, mailing lists, and discussion groups.[433]

Reasons for Internet Use

Not surprisingly, studies reveal that people use the Internet to find information. It is interesting to note that the Internet appears to be considered a good place to search for hobby information[434] or information for general interest or recreation. Searching the Web for fun is a commonly reported use of the Internet.[435] This is an interesting concept. The Internet is becoming a recreational medium or environment which people use for having fun. The World Wide Web was developed out of the computer games model of the late 1980s and early 1990s. It is interesting to note that people using the Internet are seeking fun as well as information and affiliation. Certainly, work- and study-related information seeking is an important use of the Internet, but studies are revealing that seeking problem-specific information is not as significant a using of the Internet for the general public as the search for orienting information. Orienting information is what people need for staying up to date or for monitoring daily events.[436]

Purchasing things online is also becoming a popular reason for using the Internet, particularly in the United States and Canada. The majority of people who have Internet access in the United States have purchased something online,[437] and a significant proportion of Canadians have made a purchase valued at more than $100 Canadian.[438] This trend does not necessarily follow in other countries.[439]

Gender is not a reliable predictor of Internet use by the general public. Some studies indicate that females are using the Internet more for emailing than males,[440] while other studies claim the opposite.[441] Some studies claim that women use the Internet less frequently when factors such as employment rates and education are taken into account.[442] Other studies show that gender was not a predictor of Internet use because the number of female users of the Internet is now very close to the number of male users for any typical day online.[443]

Frequency of Internet Use

In the United States, the majority of people who are using the Internet are going online every day. In the last months of 2000, for example, more than half of U.S. Internet users were online during a typical day. This represents 58 million American adults using the Internet on a daily basis.[444] Earlier studies had reported a median of five logins per week for Internet users in the United States,[445] and in Canada more than three-quarters of people in one study indicated that they were accessing the Web from home every day.[446] In Singapore the average Internet user reports browsing the World Wide Web at least a few times per week.[447] There have been some data collected that show a slight drop in Internet use in the final part of 2000. Some speculated that this might suggest a diminishing interest by the general public in using the Internet.[448] A drop in online time per day of a few minutes is not convincing evidence of a loss of interest, however. It may simply show an increase in the online efficiencies of Internet using by the general public.

Barriers to Internet Use

The barriers that prevent people from using the Internet generally relate to knowledge and cost. Some people believe that getting started on the Internet is difficult,[449] or at least somewhat difficult,[450] and yet most people who use the Internet have received no training at all on how to use the network.[451] In most cases people ask a friend for help or seek assistance from a professional colleague.[452]

Another commonly reported barrier to using the Internet for the general public user is cost. Cost, of course, does not factor into consideration where the Internet user has access to the network through the workplace or school. Here, the institution or organization bears the expense and there are economies of scale that large institutions enjoy. When it comes to everyday access to the Internet in the home, however, cost can be an important factor when deciding whether using the Internet is worthwhile. Somewhat related to cost are concerns about traffic and navigation problems.[453] Both these problems can exacerbate the cost of connecting to and using the Internet. Over time, users have reported problems using the Internet ranging from the type of personal computer that is being used to the lack of speed when moving through the network. These problems arise as a result of the facilities that individuals can afford to set up on their home computers.

Over the years, the general public has not been completely seduced by the rhetoric of immeasurable good fortune arising from using the Internet. In many cases, people are calling for realistic promotions and perceptions of the Internet. The promise of universal access to information is generally appealing, but most recognize that this will take time.[454]

Conclusion

Internet using is a very complex phenomenon. The research data that we have synthesized in this chapter provide us with a composite of micromoment perceptions of the Internet as it plays a role in the daily professional and personal lives of people. The preceding narrative is long-winded and extensively sourced because our goal is to present these data as the foundation for constructs of the Internet that can inform stakeholders who will play a role in determining how the Internet will develop. These constructs, which comprise the user's view of the Internet, are elaborated in the final chapter.

Notes

1. CERN (European Organization for Nuclear Research), "An Overview of the World Wide Web: History and Growth," http://public.web.cern.ch/Public/ACHIEVEMENTS/WEB/history.html, 3 December 1997 [accessed 12 June 2001].
2. Examples are listed in several of the following notes.
3. Adele F. Bane and William D. Milheim, "Internet Insights: How Academics Are Using the Internet," *Computers in Libraries* 15, no. 2 (1995) [this study examined 1,256 responses to a survey sent to scholarly discussion lists]; John M. Budd and Lynn Silipigni Connaway, "University Faculty and Networked Information: Results of a Survey," *Journal of the American Society for Information Science* 48, no. 9 (1997) [research participants were faculty from eight U.S. universities]; T. Matthew Ciolek, "The Scholarly Uses of the Internet: 1998 Online Survey," *Asia Web Watch: A Register of Statistical Data,* http://www.ciolek.com/PAPERS/InternetSurvey-98.html, 15 March 1998 [accessed 27 July 2001] [this study used 280 responses to a survey distributed to a variety of discussion lists]; Karen L. Curtis, Ann C. Weller, and Julie M. Hurd, "Information-Seeking Behavior of Health Sciences Faculty: The Impact of New Information Technologies," *Bulletin of the Medical Library Association* 85, no. 4 (1997) [this study examined 616 faculty in medicine, nursing, and pharmacy]; Noam Kaminer, "Scholars and the Use of the Internet," *Library and Information Science Research* 19, no. 4 (1997) [this research investigated 60 biologists and social scientists at a U.S. university]; Diane K. Kovacs, Kara L. Robinson, and Jeanne Dixon, "Scholarly E-Conferences on the Academic Networks: How Library and Information Science Professionals Use Them," *Journal of the American Society for Information Science* 46, no. 4 (1995) [this research studied 576 responses to a survey of users of library- and information science-related discussion lists]; Susan S. Lazinger, Judit Bar-Ilan, and Bluma C. Peritz, "Internet Use by Faculty Members in Various Disciplines: A Comparative Case Study," *Journal of the American Society for Information Science* 48, no. 6 (1997) [research participants were 778 faculty members at the Hebrew University of Jerusalem]; Henk J. Voorbij, "Searching Scientific Information on the Internet: A Dutch Academic User Survey," *Journal of the American Society for Information Science* 50, no. 7 (1999) [Voorbij's research examined 499 students and faculty from Dutch universities]; Yin Zhang, "Scholarly Use of Internet-Based Elec-

tronic Resources: A Survey Report," *Library Trends* 47, no. 4 (1999) [study participants were authors publishing in library and information science journals].

4. Eileen G. Abels, Peter Liebscher, and Daniel W. Denman, "Factors That Influence the Use of Electronic Networks by Science and Engineering Faculty at Small Institutions, Part I: Queries," *Journal of the American Society for Information Science* 47, no. 2 (1996) [research participants were science and engineering faculty in six small colleges in the Southeastern U.S.].

5. Harry Bruce, "Perceptions of the Internet: What People Think of When They Search the Internet for Information," *Internet Research: Electronic Networking Applications and Policy* 9, no. 3 (1999) [research participants were 37 Australian academics]; Harry Bruce, "User Satisfaction with Information Seeking on the Internet," *Journal of the American Society for Information Science* 49, no. 6 (1998) [research participants were 37 Australian academics].

6. Rick Busselle et al., "Factors Affecting Internet Use in a Saturated-Access Population," *Telematics and Informatics* 16, nos. 1-2 (1999) [research participants were faculty and staff from Washington State University].

7. Harry M. Kibirige and Lisa DePalo, "The Internet as a Source of Academic Research Information: Findings of Two Pilot Studies," *Information Technology and Libraries* 19, no. 1 (2000) [this study examined users of Internet terminals at New York academic institutions].

8. Harry Bruce, *Internet, AARNet, and Academic Work: A Longitudinal Study* (Canberra, Australia: Australian Government Publication Service, 1996).

9. Lazinger, Bar-Ilan, and Peritz, "Internet Use by Faculty Members"; Voorbij, "Searching Scientific Information on the Internet."

10. Abels, Liebscher, and Denman, "Factors That Influence the Use of Electronic Networks, Part I."

11. N. Greeve and D. E. Stanton, *AARNet Survey, 1991* (Perth, Australia: Greeve and Stanton, 1991).

12. Andrelyn Applebee et al., *Academics Online: A Nationwide Quantitative Study of Australian Academic Use of the Internet* (Adelaide, Australia: Auslib Press, 1998); Budd and Connaway, "University Faculty and Networked Information"; Kaminer, "Scholars and the Use of the Internet."

13. Kaminer, "Scholars and the Use of the Internet."

14. Zhang, "Scholarly Use of Internet-Based Electronic Resources."

15. Kibirige and DePalo, "The Internet as a Source."

16. Budd and Connaway, "University Faculty and Networked Information."

17. Ciolek, "Scholarly Uses of the Internet."

18. Voorbij, "Searching Scientific Information on the Internet."

19. Lazinger, Bar-Ilan, and Peritz, "Internet Use by Faculty Members."

20. Abels, Liebscher, and Denman, "Factors That Influence the Use of Electronic Networks, Part I."

21. Abels, Liebscher, and Denman, "Factors That Influence the Use of Electronic Networks, Part I."

22. Voorbij, "Searching Scientific Information on the Internet."

23. Abels, Liebscher, and Denman, "Factors That Influence the Use of Electronic Networks, Part I."

24. Abels, Liebscher, and Denman, "Factors That Influence the Use of Electronic Networks, Part I."

25. Applebee et al., *Academics Online;* Bruce, *Internet, AARNet and Academic Work.*

26. Bane and Milheim, "Internet Insights."

27. Zhang, "Scholarly Use of Internet-Based Electronic Resources."

28. Kaminer, "Scholars and the Use of the Internet."

29. Voorbij, "Searching Scientific Information on the Internet."

30. Charles R. McClure et al., *The National Research and Education Network (NREN): Research and Policy Perspectives* (Norwood, N.J.: Ablex Publishing, 1991); Charles R. McClure, William E. Moen, and J. Ryan, "Academic Libraries and the Impact of Internet/NREN: Key Issues and Findings," (paper presented at the 56th Annual Meeting of the American Society for Information Science, 1993).

31. Applebee et al., *Academics Online*; Harry Bruce, "Internet Services and Academic Work: An Australian Perspective," *Internet Research: Electronic Networking Applications and Policy* 4, no. 2 (1994); Bruce, *Internet, AARNet, and Academic Work;* Bruce, "User Satisfaction with Information Seeking on the Internet."

32. Voorbij, "Searching Scientific Information on the Internet."

33. Brian R. Gaines, Lee Li-Jen Chen, and Mildred L. G. Shaw, "Modeling the Human Factors of Scholarly Communities Supported through the Internet and World Wide Web," *Journal of the American Society for Information Science* 48, no. 11 (1997).

34. Lazinger, Bar-Ilan, and Peritz, "Internet Use by Faculty Members."

35. Wendy Shaw, "The Use of the Internet by English Academics," *Information Research*, http://www.shef.ac.uk/~is/publications/infres/isic/shaw.html, 3 February 1999 [accessed 15 May 2001].

36. Bruce, "Internet Services and Academic Work"; Bruce, *Internet, AARNet, and Academic Work;* Bruce, "User Satisfaction with Information Seeking on the Internet."

37. Bruce, "Internet Services and Academic Work," 32-33.

38. Applebee et al., *Academics Online.*

39. Voorbij, "Searching Scientific Information on the Internet."

40. Lazinger, Bar-Ilan, and Peritz, "Internet Use by Faculty Members."

41. Abels, Liebscher, and Denman, "Factors That Influence the Use of Electronic Networks, Part I"; Bane and Milheim, "Internet Insights"; Curtis, Weller, and Hurd, "Information-Seeking Behavior of Health Sciences Faculty"; Peter Liebscher, Eileen G. Abels, and Daniel W. Denman, "Factors That Influence the Use of Electronic Networks by Science and Engineering Faculty at Small Institutions, Part II: Preliminary Use Indicators," *Journal of the American Society for Information Science* 48, no. 6 (1997); Voorbij, "Searching Scientific Information on the Internet."

42. Zhang, "Scholarly Use of Internet-Based Electronic Resources."

43. Ciolek, "Scholarly Uses of the Internet."

44. Liebscher, Abels, and Denman, "Factors That Influence the Use of Electronic Networks, Part II."

45. Kovacs, Robinson, and Dixon, "Scholarly E-Conferences on the Academic Networks."

46. Bruce, "Internet Services and Academic Work."

47. Liebscher, Abels, and Denman, "Factors That Influence the Use of Electronic Networks, Part II."

48. Lazinger, Bar-Ilan, and Peritz, "Internet Use by Faculty Members."

49. Liebscher, Abels, and Denman, "Factors That Influence the Use of Electronic Networks, Part II."

50. Abels, Liebscher, and Denman, "Factors That Influence the Use of Electronic Networks, Part I."

51. Zhang, "Scholarly Use of Internet-Based Electronic Resources."

52. Bane and Milheim, "Internet Insights."

53. Curtis, Weller, and Hurd, "Information Seeking-Behavior of Health Sciences Faculty."

54. Liebscher, Abels, and Denman, "Factors That Influence the Use of Electronic Networks, Part II."

55. Applebee et al., *Academics Online.*

56. Kovacs, Robinson, and Dixon, "Scholarly E-Conferences on the Academic Networks."

57. Applebee et al., *Academics Online.*

58. Budd and Connaway, "University Faculty and Networked Information."

59. Budd and Connaway, "University Faculty and Networked Information."

60. Bane and Milheim, "Internet Insights"; Voorbij, "Searching Scientific Information on the Internet."

61. Budd and Connaway, "University Faculty and Networked Information."

62. Voorbij, "Searching Scientific Information on the Internet."

63. Zhang, "Scholarly Use of Internet-Based Electronic Resources."

64. Applebee et al., *Academics Online;* Zhang, "Scholarly Use of Internet-Based Electronic Resources."

65. Zhang, "Scholarly Use of Internet-Based Electronic Resources."

66. Voorbij, "Searching Scientific Information on the Internet."

67. Bruce, "User Satisfaction with Information Seeking on the Internet."

68. Liebscher, Abels, and Denman, "Factors That Influence the Use of Electronic Networks, Part II."

69. Zhang, "Scholarly Use of Internet-Based Electronic Resources."

70. Liebscher, Abels, and Denman, "Factors That Influence the Use of Electronic Networks, Part II"; Zhang, "Scholarly Use of Internet-Based Electronic Resources."

71. Applebee et al., *Academics Online.*

72. Lazinger, Bar-Ilan, and Peritz, "Internet Use by Faculty Members"; Voorbij, "Searching Scientific Information on the Internet."

73. Bruce, "User Satisfaction with Information Seeking on the Internet."

74. Abels, Liebscher, and Denman, "Factors That Influence the Use of Electronic Networks, Part I."

75. Bruce, *Internet, AARNet, and Academic Work.*

76. Bruce, "User Satisfaction with Information Seeking on the Internet."

77. Busselle et al., "Factors Affecting Internet Use."

78. Kaminer, "Scholars and the Use of the Internet."

79. Busselle et al., "Factors Affecting Internet Use."

80. Kaminer, "Scholars and the Use of the Internet."

81. Kibirige and DePalo, "The Internet as a Source."

82. Ciolek, "Scholarly Uses of the Internet."

83. Abels, Liebscher, and Denman, "Factors That Influence the Use of Electronic Networks, Part I."

84. Bruce, "User Satisfaction with Information Seeking on the Internet"; Bruce, "Perceptions of the Internet"; Voorbij, "Searching Scientific Information on the Internet."

85. Voorbij, "Searching Scientific Information on the Internet."

86. Voorbij, "Searching Scientific Information on the Internet."

87. Bruce, "User Satisfaction with Information Seeking on the Internet"; Bruce, "Perceptions of the Internet."

88. Hilary Yerbury and Joan Parker, "Novice Searchers' Use of Familiar Structures in Searching Bibliographic Information Retrieval Systems," *Journal of Information Science* 24, no. 4 (1998).

89. Bruce, "Perceptions of the Internet."

90. Kaba Abdoulaye and Shaheen Majid, "Use of the Internet for Reference Services in Malaysian Academic Libraries," *Online Information Review* 24, no. 5 (2000) [research participants were 40 Malaysian academic reference librarians]; Justin Chisenga, "A Study of the Use of the Internet among Library Professionals in Sub-Saharan Africa," *Internet Reference Services Quarterly* 4, no. 1 (1999) [study examined responses of 47 librarians in Sub-Saharan Africa]; Karen Finlay and Thomas Finlay, "The Relative Roles of Knowledge and Innovativeness in Determining Librarians' Attitudes toward and Use of the Internet: A Structural Equation Modeling Approach," *Library Quarterly* 66, no. 1 (1996) [101 Canadian librarians participated in the research]; Rochelle Logan, "Colorado Librarian Internet Use: Results of a Survey," *School Library Media Quarterly*, http://www.ala.org/aasl/SLMQ/logan.html, 1998 [accessed 21 October 2000] [a total of 116 public and school librarians participated in this research]; Truda Olson, "University Reference Librarians Using Internet: A Survey," *Australian Academic and Research Libraries* 26, no. 3 (1995) [study participants were 130 Australian academic reference librarians]; Sue Pettit, "Internet Use by U.K. Academic Law Librarians," *Law Librarian* 26, no. 1 (1995) [this research examined U.K. academic law librarians]; Marilyn Rosenthal and Marsha Spiegelman, "Evaluating Use of the Internet among Academic Reference Librarians," *Internet Reference Services Quarterly* 1, no. 1

(1996) [research examined 139 librarians drawn from a list of college and research librarians in the Northeastern U.S.]; Joanna Scarlett, "Internet Use Survey," *Law Librarian* 28, no. 2 (1997) [research examined 68 legal information professionals worldwide]; Gerry Smith, "Business Librarians Embrace the Internet: Annual Business Information Resources Survey," *Business Information Review* 14, no. 1 (1997) [study participants were 159 U.K. business librarians]; Mark Stover, "Reference Librarians and the Internet: A Qualitative Study," *Reference Services Review* 28, no. 1 (2000) [this study examined 41 respondents from a website and listserv].

91. Harry Bruce and Peter Clayton, "An Internet Role for the Academic Librarian?" *Australian Academic and Research Libraries* 30, no. 3 (1999).

92. Sarah Kelly and David Nicholas, "Is the Business Cybrarian a Reality? Internet Use in Business Libraries," *ASLIB Proceedings* 48, no. 5 (1996) [study examined information professionals in the U.K. banking and finance sector]; Jane E. Klobas, "Networked Information Resources: Electronic Opportunities for Users and Librarians," *OCLC Systems and Services* 13, no. 1 (1997) [research participants were academic faculty and staff].

93. Stover, "Reference Librarians and the Internet."

94. Pettit, "Internet Use by U.K. Academic Law Librarians."

95. Abdoulaye and Majid, "Use of the Internet in Malaysian Libraries."

96. Logan, "Colorado Librarian Internet Use."

97. Smith, "Business Librarians Embrace the Internet."

98. Kelly and Nicholas, "Is the Business Cybrarian a Reality?"

99. Chisenga, "Use of the Internet in Sub-Saharan Africa."

100. Rosenthal and Spiegelman, "Evaluating Use of the Internet."

101. Finlay and Finlay, "The Relative Roles of Knowledge and Innovativeness," 66.

102. Logan, "Colorado Librarian Internet Use."

103. Scarlett, "Internet Use Survey."

104. Pettit, "Internet Use by U.K. Academic Law Librarians."

105. Logan, "Colorado Librarian Internet Use."

106. Pettit, "Internet Use by U.K. Academic Law Librarians."

107. Chisenga, "Use of the Internet in Sub-Saharan Africa."

108. Logan, "Colorado Librarian Internet Use."

109. Chisenga, "Use of the Internet in Sub-Saharan Africa."

110. Chisenga, "Use of the Internet in Sub-Saharan Africa."

111. Logan, "Colorado Librarian Internet Use"; Olson, "University Reference Librarians Using Internet."

112. Abdoulaye and Majid, "Use of the Internet in Malaysian Libraries"; Logan, "Colorado Librarian Internet Use."

113. Rosenthal and Spiegelman, "Evaluating Use of the Internet."

114. Kelly and Nicholas, "Is the Business Cybrarian a Reality?"; Scarlett, "Internet Use Survey," 103.

115. Stover, "Reference Librarians and the Internet."

116. Pettit, "Internet Use by U.K. Academic Law Librarians."

117. Rosenthal and Spiegelman, "Evaluating Use of the Internet."

118. Abdoulaye and Majid, "Use of the Internet in Malaysian Libraries."

119. Rosenthal and Spiegelman, "Evaluating Use of the Internet."

120. Abdoulaye and Majid, "Use of the Internet in Malaysian Libraries."

121. Finlay and Finlay, "The Relative Roles of Knowledge and Innovativeness."

122. Finlay and Finlay, "The Relative Roles of Knowledge and Innovativeness."

123. Logan, "Colorado Librarian Internet Use."

124. Finlay and Finlay, "The Relative Roles of Knowledge and Innovativeness."

125. Finlay and Finlay, "The Relative Roles of Knowledge and Innovativeness."

126. Olson, "University Reference Librarians Using Internet."

127. Abdoulaye and Majid, "Use of the Internet in Malaysian Libraries"; Rosenthal and Spiegelman, "Evaluating Use of the Internet."

128. Stover, "Reference Librarians and the Internet."

129. Rosenthal and Spiegelman, "Evaluating Use of the Internet."

130. Logan, "Colorado Librarian Internet Use."

131. Stover, "Reference Librarians and the Internet."

132. Logan, "Colorado Librarian Internet Use"; Rosenthal and Spiegelman, "Evaluating Use of the Internet."

133. Kelly and Nicholas, "Is the Business Cybrarian a Reality?"

134. Logan, "Colorado Librarian Internet Use"; Rosenthal and Spiegelman, "Evaluating Use of the Internet."

135. Kelly and Nicholas, "Is the Business Cybrarian a Reality?"; Logan, "Colorado Librarian Internet Use."

136. Abdoulaye and Majid, "Use of the Internet in Malaysian Libraries."

137. Logan, "Colorado Librarian Internet Use."

138. Kelly and Nicholas, "Is the Business Cybrarian a Reality?"

139. Abdoulaye and Majid, "Use of the Internet in Malaysian Libraries."

140. Stover, "Reference Librarians and the Internet."

141. Scarlett, "Internet Use Survey."

142. Kelly and Nicholas, "Is the Business Cybrarian a Reality?"; Stover, "Reference Librarians and the Internet."

143. Scarlett, "Internet Use Survey."

144. Chisenga, "Use of the Internet in Sub-Saharan Africa"; Kelly and Nicholas, "Is the Business Cybrarian a Reality?"; Scarlett, "Internet Use Survey."

145. Chisenga, "Use of the Internet in Sub-Saharan Africa."

146. Scarlett, "Internet Use Survey."

147. Kelly and Nicholas, "Is the Business Cybrarian a Reality?"

148. Chisenga, "Use of the Internet in Sub-Saharan Africa"; Pettit, "Internet Use by U.K. Academic Law Librarians."

149. Chisenga, "Use of the Internet in Sub-Saharan Africa"; Scarlett, "Internet Use Survey."

150. Olson, "University Reference Librarians Using Internet."

151. Abdoulaye and Majid, "Use of the Internet in Malaysian Libraries."

152. Bruce and Clayton, "An Internet Role for the Academic Librarian?"

153. Voorbij, "Searching Scientific Information on the Internet."

154. See Carol Collier Kuhlthau, "Inside the Search Process: Information Seeking from the User's Perspective," *Journal of the American Society for Information Science* 42, no. 5 (1991).

155. Xue-Ming Bao, "Challenges and Opportunities: A Report of the 1998 Library Survey of Internet Users at Seton Hall University," *College and Research Libraries* 59, no. 6 (1998) [this study examined 786 students]; Phyllis Blumberg and JoAnne Sparks, "Tracing the Evolution of Critical Evaluation Skills in Students' Use of the Internet," *Bulletin of the Medical Library Association* 87, no. 2 (1999) [research participants were 25 students in a graduate public health program]; Chien Chou and Ming-Chun Hsiao, "Internet Addiction, Usage, Gratification, and Pleasure Experience: The Taiwan College Students' Case," *Computers and Education* 35 (2000) [this study examined 910 Taiwanese college students]; Peter Wei He and Trudi E. Jacobson, "What Are They Doing with the Internet? A Study of User Information Seeking Behaviors," *Internet Reference Quarterly* 1, no. 1 (1996) [study examined responses of 96 patrons using Internet terminals];

Felicia Mitchell, "Internet Use and Gender and Emory and Henry College: A Survey of Student Users," *College and Undergraduate Libraries* 5, no. 2 (1998) [research participants were 52 students using Kelly Library at Emory and Henry University in Virginia]; J. Morahan-Martin and P. Schumacher, "Incidence and Correlates of Pathological Internet Use among College Students," *Computers in Human Behavior* 16, no. 1 (2000) [this study examined 277 undergraduates in courses requiring Internet use]; Nancy L. Pelzer, William H. Wiese, and Joan M. Leysen, "Library Use and Information-Seeking Behavior of Veterinary Medical Students Revisited in the Electronic Environment," *Bulletin of the Medical Library Association* 86, no. 3 (1998) [398 research participants from university veterinary school]; Kathy Scherer, "College Life On-Line: Healthy and Unhealthy Internet Use," *Journal of College Student Development* 38, no. 6 (1997) [this study examined a random sample of 531 students at the University of Texas at Austin]; Melanie Ward and David Newlands, "Use of the Web in Undergraduate Teaching," *Computers and Education* 31, no. 2 (1998) [53 undergraduate students from an honors economics class at Aberdeen University participated in this study].

156. Nigel Ford and Dave Miller, "Gender Differences in Internet Perception and Use," *ASLIB Proceedings* 48, no. 7/8 (July/August 1996) [this study examined 117 students at Sheffield University in the U.K.]; John Lubans, Jr., "How First-Year University Students Use and Regard Internet Resources," *Duke University*, http://www.lib.duke.edu/lubans/docs/1styear/firstyear.html, 8 April 1998 [accessed 12 December 2000] [research examined 235 responses of users in campus libraries].

157. Joanne E. D'Esposito and Rachel M. Gardner, "University Students' Perceptions of the Internet: An Exploratory Study," *Journal of Academic Librarianship* 25, no. 6 (1999) [14 students from Monmouth University in New Jersey participated in this research].

158. Janette R. Hill, "The World Wide Web as a Tool for Information Retrieval: An Exploratory Study of Users' Strategies in an Open-Ended System," *School Library Media Quarterly* 25 (Summer 1997) [this study examined 10 students from an introductory course in technology].

159. Timothy T. Perry, Leslie Anne Perry, and Karen Hosack-Curlin, "Internet Use by University Students: An Interdisciplinary Study on Three Campuses," *Internet Research: Electronic Networking Applications and Policy* 8, no. 2 (1998) [research participants were 548 students in 21 classes at three Southeastern U.S. universities].

160. Scherer, "College Life On-Line."

161. Bao, "Challenges and Opportunities"; Lubans, "How Students Use and Regard Internet Resources."

162. Scherer, "College Life On-Line."

163. James E. Pitkow and Colleen M. Kehoe, "Results from the Graphics, Visualization, and Usability Center's Fourth WWW User Survey," *GVU User Surveys,* http://www.cc.gatech.edu/GVU/user_surveys/survey-10-1995/, 1995 [accessed 8 June 2001].

164. Perry, Perry, and Hosack-Curlin, "Internet Use by University Students."

165. Scherer, "College Life On-Line."

166. Mitchell, "Internet Use and Gender."

167. Lubans, "How Students Use and Regard Internet Resources."

168. Mitchell, "Internet Use and Gender."

169. He and Jacobson, "What Are They Doing with the Internet?"

170. Mitchell, "Internet Use and Gender."

171. Perry, Perry, and Hosack-Curlin, "Internet Use by University Students"; Scherer, "College Life On-Line."

172. Scherer, "College Life On-Line."

173. He and Jacobson, "What Are They Doing with the Internet?"

174. Scherer, "College Life On-Line."

175. Perry, Perry, and Hosack-Curlin, "Internet Use by University Students."

176. Perry, Perry, and Hosack-Curlin, "Internet Use by University Students."

177. Ward and Newlands, "Use of the Web in Teaching."

178. Bao, "Challenges and Opportunities."

179. Scherer, "College Life On-Line."

180. Ford and Miller, "Gender Differences in Internet Perception"; Mitchell, "Internet Use and Gender."

181. Mitchell, "Internet Use and Gender."

182. Morahan-Martin and Schumacher, "Incidence and Correlates of Pathological Internet Use."

183. Jonathan J. Kandell, "Internet Addiction on Campus: The Vulnerability of College Students," *CyberPsychology and Behavior* 1, no. 1 (1998).

184. Chou and Hsiao, "Internet Addiction."

185. Chou and Hsiao, "Internet Addiction."

186. Morahan-Martin and Schumacher, "Incidence and Correlates of Pathological Internet Use."

187. Scherer, "College Life On-Line."

188. Scherer, "College Life On-Line."

189. Morahan-Martin and Schumacher, "Incidence and Correlates of Pathological Internet Use."

190. Morahan-Martin and Schumacher, "Incidence and Correlates of Pathological Internet Use"; Scherer, "College Life On-Line."

191. Morahan-Martin and Schumacher, "Incidence and Correlates of Pathological Internet Use."

192. Chou and Hsiao, "Internet Addiction."

193. He and Jacobson, "What Are They Doing with the Internet?"

194. Lubans, "How Students Use and Regard Internet Resources."

195. Scherer, "College Life On-Line."

196. He and Jacobson, "What Are They Doing with the Internet?"

197. Pelzer, Wiese, and Leysen, "Library Use and Information-Seeking Behavior."

198. Blumberg and Sparks, "Tracing the Evolution of Skills."

199. Ford and Miller, "Gender Differences in Internet Perception."

200. Hill, "The World Wide Web as a Tool."

201. Ford and Miller, "Gender Differences in Internet Perception."

202. D'Esposito and Gardner, "University Students' Perceptions of the Internet."

203. D'Esposito and Gardner, "University Students' Perceptions of the Internet."

204. D'Esposito and Gardner, "University Students' Perceptions of the Internet."

205. Bao, "Challenges and Opportunities."

206. Blumberg and Sparks, "Tracing the Evolution of Skills"; He and Jacobson, "What Are They Doing with the Internet?"

207. Pelzer, Wiese, and Leysen, "Library Use and Information-Seeking Behavior."

208. Blumberg and Sparks, "Tracing the Evolution of Skills"; D'Esposito and Gardner, "University Students' Perceptions of the Internet."

209. D'Esposito and Gardner, "University Students' Perceptions of the Internet."

210. Henry Jay Becker, "Internet Use by Teachers: Conditions of Professional Use and Teacher-Directed Student Use" (Irvine, Calif.: Center for Research on Information Technology and Organizations, 1999) [this research investigated approximately 2,250 teachers of fourth to twelfth grade classes in U.S. public and private schools]; Henry J. Becker and Jason Ravitz, "The Influence of Computer and Internet Use on Teachers' Pedagogical Practices and Perceptions,"

Journal of Research on Computing in Education 31, no. 4 (1999) [441 teachers employed in U.S. elementary and secondary schools participated in this research]; Lisa Hack and Sue Smey, "A Survey of Internet Use by Teachers in Three Urban Connecticut Schools," *School Library Media Quarterly* 25, no. 3 (1997) [this study examined 102 teachers in three Connecticut public schools]; Jon M. Peha, "How K-12 Teachers Are Using Computer Networks," *Educational Leadership* 53, no. 2 (1995) [35 teachers from the Pittsburgh area participated in this research]; Phillip J. Vanfossen, "Degree of Internet/WWW Use and Barriers to Use among Secondary Social Studies Teachers," *International Journal of Instructional Media* 28, no. 1 (2001) [this study investigated a random sample of 350 social studies teachers in the state of Indiana]; Randall L. Wiesenmayer and George R. Meadows, "Addressing Science Teachers' Initial Perceptions of the Classroom Uses of Internet and World Wide Web-Based Resource Materials," *Journal of Science Education and Technology* 6, no. 4 (1997) [288 West Virginia science and mathematics teachers participated in this research].

211. Judith B. Harris and Neal Grandgenett, "Correlates with Use of Telecomputing Tools: K-12 Teachers' Beliefs and Demographics," *Journal of Research on Computing in Education* 31, no. 4 (1999) [this study examined teachers holding telnet accounts].

212. Michael A. Gallo and Phillip B. Horton, "Direct and Unrestricted Access to the Internet: A Case Study of an East Central Florida High School," *Educational Technology Research and Development* 42, no. 4 (1994) [study investigated teachers at seven high schools in East Central Florida].

213. Cassandra Rowand, "Teacher Use of Computers and the Internet in Public Schools: Stats in Brief," (Washington, D.C.: National Center for Education Statistics, 2000).

214. Vanfossen, "Degree of Internet/WWW Use."

215. Hack and Smey, "Internet Use by Teachers in Connecticut."

216. Hack and Smey, "Internet Use by Teachers in Connecticut"; Rowand, "Teacher Use of Computers and the Internet."

217. Hack and Smey, "Internet Use by Teachers in Connecticut."

218. Becker, "Internet Use by Teachers"; Vanfossen, "Degree of Internet/WWW Use."

219. Becker, "Internet Use by Teachers"; Hack and Smey, "Internet Use by Teachers in Connecticut."

220. Becker, "Internet Use by Teachers"; Hack and Smey, "Internet Use by Teachers in Connecticut"; Vanfossen, "Degree of Internet/WWW Use."

221. Hack and Smey, "Internet Use by Teachers in Connecticut"; Vanfossen, "Degree of Internet/WWW Use."

222. Harris and Grandgenett, "Correlates with Use of Telecomputing Tools: K-12 Teachers' Beliefs and Demographics."

223. Becker, "Internet Use by Teachers: Conditions of Professional Use and Teacher-Directed Student Use."

224. Becker, "Internet Use by Teachers: Conditions of Professional Use and Teacher-Directed Student Use"; Hack and Smey, "A Survey of Internet Use by Teachers in Three Urban Connecticut Schools."

225. Harris and Grandgenett, "Correlates with Use of Telecomputing Tools."

226. Vanfossen, "Degree of Internet/WWW Use."

227. Susan Gibson and Dianne Oberg, "Learning to Use the Internet: A Study of Teacher Learning through Collaborative Research Partnerships," *Alberta Journal of Educational Research* 44, no. 2 (1998) [this research examined six teachers].

228. Becker, "Internet Use by Teachers"; Vanfossen, "Degree of Internet/WWW Use."

229. Rowand, "Teacher Use of Computers and the Internet."

230. Becker, "Internet Use by Teachers"; Vanfossen, "Degree of Internet/WWW Use."

231. Hack and Smey, "Internet Use by Teachers in Connecticut"; Vanfossen, "Degree of Internet/WWW Use."

232. Gallo and Horton, "Direct and Unrestricted Access to the Internet."

233. Becker, "Internet Use by Teachers"; Wiesenmayer and Meadows, "Addressing Science Teachers' Perceptions."

234. Vanfossen, "Degree of Internet/WWW Use."

235. Becker, "Internet Use by Teachers."

236. Becker, "Internet Use by Teachers."

237. Hack and Smey, "Internet Use by Teachers in Connecticut"; Rowand, "Teacher Use of Computers and the Internet."

238. Becker, "Internet Use by Teachers"; Vanfossen, "Degree of Internet/WWW Use."

239. Becker, "Internet Use by Teachers."

240. Harris and Grandgenett, "Correlates with Use of Telecomputing Tools."

241. Harris and Grandgenett, "Correlates with Use of Telecomputing Tools."

242. Hack and Smey, "Internet Use by Teachers in Connecticut."

243. Becker, "Internet Use by Teachers"; Vanfossen, "Degree of Internet/WWW Use."

244. Gallo and Horton, "Direct and Unrestricted Access to the Internet."

245. Becker, "Internet Use by Teachers."

246. Becker, "Internet Use by Teachers."

247. Becker, "Internet Use by Teachers."

248. Becker, "Internet Use by Teachers."

249. Becker and Ravitz, "Influence of Internet Use on Teachers."

250. Becker and Ravitz, "Influence of Internet Use on Teachers."

251. Harris and Grandgenett, "Correlates with Use of Telecomputing Tools."

252. Becker, "Internet Use by Teachers."

253. Gallo and Horton, "Direct and Unrestricted Access to the Internet."

254. Gibson and Oberg, "Learning to Use the Internet."

255. Gallo and Horton, "Direct and Unrestricted Access to the Internet."

256. Becker and Ravitz, "Influence of Internet Use on Teachers."

257. Becker, "Internet Use by Teachers."

258. Hack and Smey, "Internet Use by Teachers in Connecticut."

259. Becker, "Internet Use by Teachers."

260. Peha, "How K-12 Teachers Are Using Computer Networks."

261. Hack and Smey, "Internet Use by Teachers in Connecticut"; Peha, "How K-12 Teachers Are Using Computer Networks."

262. Becker, "Internet Use by Teachers."

263. Rowand, "Teacher Use of Computers and the Internet."

264. Vanfossen, "Degree of Internet/WWW Use."

265. Gallo and Horton, "Direct and Unrestricted Access to the Internet."

266. Gibson and Oberg, "Learning to Use the Internet"; Peha, "How K-12 Teachers Are Using Computer Networks."

267. Vanfossen, "Degree of Internet/WWW Use."

268. Rowand, "Teacher Use of Computers and the Internet."

269. Peha, "How K-12 Teachers Are Using Computer Networks."

270. Becker, "Internet Use by Teachers."

271. Gibson and Oberg, "Learning to Use the Internet."

272. Peha, "How K-12 Teachers Are Using Computer Networks."

273. Wiesenmayer and Meadows, "Addressing Science Teachers' Perceptions."

274. Vanfossen, "Degree of Internet/WWW Use."

275. Becker, "Internet Use by Teachers"; Hack and Smey, "Internet Use by Teachers in Connecticut."

276. Yasmin B. Kafai and Sharon Sutton, "Elementary School Students' Computer and Internet Use at Home: Current Trends and Issues," *Journal of Educational Computing Research* 21, no. 3 (1999) [357 students at a laboratory school at a California public university participated in this study]; Carrie LaFerle, Steven M. Edwards, and Wei-Na Lee, "Teens' Use of Traditional Media and the Internet," *Journal of Advertising Research* 40, no. 3 (2000) [this research examined 189 mostly Caucasian and middle-class students at a southwestern U.S. high school]; Rafi Nachmias, David Mioduser, and Anat Shemla, "Internet Usage by Students in an Israeli High School," *Journal of Educational Computing Research* 22, no. 1 (2000) [384 Tel-Aviv high school student participated in this research]; S. H. Wee, "Internet Use amongst Secondary School Students in Kuala Lumpur, Malaysia," *Malaysian Journal of Library and Information Science* 4, no. 2 (1999) [608 high school-age students in Kuala Lumpur, Malaysia, participated in this study].

277. Dania Bilal, "Children's Use of the Yahooligans! Web Search Engine 1," part: "Cognitive, Physical, and Affective Behaviors on Fact-Based Search Tasks," *Journal of the American Society for Information Science* 51, no. 7 (2000) [research examined 22 students at a middle school in Knoxville, Tennessee]; Steve Coffey and Horst Stipp, "The Interactions between Computer and Television Usage," *Journal of Advertising Research* 37, no. 2 (1997) [Coffey and Stipp polled 10,076 households]; Christian Sandvig, "The Internet Disconnect in Children's Policy: A User Study of Outcomes for Internet Access Subsidies and Content Regulation" (paper presented at the 28th Conference on Communication, Information, and Internet Policy, Alexandria, Virginia, 2000) [study examined visitors to a children's center at San Francisco Public Library's main library]; John Schacter, Gregory K. W. K. Chung, and Aimee Dorr, "Children's Internet Searching on Complex Problems: Performance and Process Analyses," *Journal of the American Society for Information Science* 49, no. 9 (1998) [32 fifth- and sixth-grade students from a laboratory school at a California university participated in this study].

278. Raya Fidel et al., "A Visit to the Information Mall: Web Searching Behavior of High School Students," *Journal of the American Society for Information Science* 50, no. 1 (1999) [Fidel et al. examined eight students at West Seattle High School in Seattle, Washington]; Shelley Martin, "Internet Use in the Classroom: The Impact of Gen-

der," *Social Science Computer Review* 16, no. 4 (1998) [this research investigated 30 students ages 8 to 10 in Canada]; Peter Williams, "The Net Generation: The Experiences, Attitudes and Behaviour of Children Using the Internet for Their Own Purposes," *ASLIB Proceedings* 51, no. 9 (1999) [research participants were students at a primary school in Hertford, England].

279. R. Kraut et al., "The Home Net Field Trial of Residential Internet Services," *Communications of the ACM* 39, no. 12 (1996) [48 families recruited through four demographically diverse high schools in Pittsburgh, Pennsylvania participated in this study; families were lent or sold a computer with modem]; John Lubans, "Key Findings on Internet Use among Students," *Duke University*, http://www.lib.duke.edu/lubans/docs/key/key.html, 5 March 1999, [accessed 13 May 2001]; John Lubans, Jr., "When Students Hit the Surf: What Kids Really Do on the Internet and What They Want from Librarians," *School Library Journal* (September 1999) [both Lubans studies examined 226 seventh to tenth grade students that spent the summer at Duke University].

280. Kafai and Sutton, "Elementary Students' Internet Use at Home"; Wee, "Internet Use in Kuala Lumpur."

281. Kafai and Sutton, "Elementary Students' Internet Use at Home."

282. Kraut et al., "The Home Net Field Trial"; Wee, "Internet Use in Kuala Lumpur."

283. Coffey and Stipp, "The Interactions between Computer and Television Usage"; LaFerle, Edwards, and Lee, "Teens' Use of Traditional Media and the Internet"; Nachmias, Mioduser, and Shemla, "Internet Usage in an Israeli High School."

284. Wee, "Internet Use in Kuala Lumpur."

285. Nachmias, Mioduser, and Shemla, "Internet Usage in an Israeli High School."

286. LaFerle, Edwards, and Lee, "Teens' Use of Traditional Media and the Internet."

287. Kraut et al., "The Home Net Field Trial"; Nachmias, Mioduser, and Shemla, "Internet Usage in an Israeli High School."

288. Kraut et al., "The Home Net Field Trial."

289. Coffey and Stipp, "The Interactions between Computer and Television Usage."

290. Lubans, "Key Findings on Internet Use among Students."

291. Kraut et al., "The Home Net Field Trial."

292. Kraut et al., "The Home Net Field Trial."

293. Nachmias, Mioduser, and Shemla, "Internet Usage in an Israeli High School"; Wee, "Internet Use in Kuala Lumpur."

294. Lubans, "Key Findings on Internet Use among Students."

295. Williams, "The Net Generation."

296. Nachmias, Mioduser, and Shemla, "Internet Usage in an Israeli High School."

297. LaFerle, Edwards, and Lee, "Teens' Use of Traditional Media and the Internet."

298. Kafai and Sutton, "Elementary Students' Internet Use at Home."

299. Nachmias, Mioduser, and Shemla, "Internet Usage in an Israeli High School"; Wee, "Internet Use in Kuala Lumpur."

300. Nachmias, Mioduser, and Shemla, "Internet Usage in an Israeli High School."

301. Kraut et al., "The Home Net Field Trial."

302. Sandvig, "The Internet Disconnect in Children's Policy."

303. Sandvig, "The Internet Disconnect in Children's Policy."

304. Williams, "The Net Generation."

305. Sandvig, "The Internet Disconnect in Children's Policy."

306. Sandvig, "The Internet Disconnect in Children's Policy"; Williams, "The Net Generation."

307. Williams, "The Net Generation."

308. Wee, "Internet Use in Kuala Lumpur."

309. Sandvig, "The Internet Disconnect in Children's Policy"; Williams, "The Net Generation."

310. LaFerle, Edwards, and Lee, "Teens' Use of Traditional Media and the Internet."

311. LaFerle, Edwards, and Lee, "Teens' Use of Traditional Media and the Internet."

312. Martin, "Internet Use in the Classroom."

313. LaFerle, Edwards, and Lee, "Teens' Use of Traditional Media and the Internet."

314. Fidel et al., "A Visit to the Information Mall."

315. Wee, "Internet Use in Kuala Lumpur."

316. Fidel et al., "A Visit to the Information Mall"; Wee, "Internet Use in Kuala Lumpur."

317. Schacter, Chung, and Dorr, "Children's Internet Searching."

318. Lubans, "Key Findings on Internet Use among Students."

319. Williams, "The Net Generation."

320. Fidel et al., "A Visit to the Information Mall"; Schacter, Chung, and Dorr, "Children's Internet Searching."

321. Eliza T. Dresang, "More Research Needed: Informal Information-Seeking Behavior of Youth on the Internet," *Journal of the American Society for Information Science* 50, no. 12 (1999).

322. Schacter, Chung, and Dorr, "Children's Internet Searching."

323. Fidel et al., "A Visit to the Information Mall."

324. Schacter, Chung, and Dorr, "Children's Internet Searching."

325. S. K. Wyman et al., "Developing System-Based and User-Based Criteria for Assessing Federal Web Sites" (paper presented at the 60th Annual Meeting of the American Society for Information Science, 1997).

326. Brenda Dervin, "Information (If and Only If) Democracy: An Examination of Underlying Assumptions," *Journal of the American Society for Information Science* 45, no. 6 (1994), 369.

327. Steven R. Corman, "Use and Uses of a Congressman's Network Information Services," *Internet Research: Electronic Networking Applications and Policy* 4, no. 4 (1994) [78 individuals on U.S. Representative Sam Coppersmith's email distribution list participated in this research].

328. "No Gain without Pain: Why the Transition to E-Government Will Hurt," *Economist*, June 22, 2000.

329. Ching-Shyang Hwang, "A Comparative Study of Tax-Filing Methods: Manual, Internet, and Two-Dimensional Bar Code," *Journal of Government Information* 27, no. 2 (2000) [30 Taiwanese taxpayers and 30 Taiwanese students participated in this experiment; 400 Taiwanese citizens participated in follow-up questionnaire].

330. Bruce Bimber, "The Internet and Political Mobilization: Research Note on the 1996 Election Season," *Social Science Computer Review* 16, no. 4 (1998) [this research had a total of 5,560 respondents].

331. Corman, "Use and Uses of a Congressman's Network."

332. Andrea Ricci, "Towards a Systematic Study of Internet-Based Political and Social Communication in Europe," *Telematics and Informatics* 15, no. 3 (1998) [approximately 500 people representative of European Union member states participated in this research].

333. Lynn Burke, "The Tangled Web of E-Voting," *Wired.com*, http://wired.com/news/print/0,1294,37050,00.htm, 26 June 2000 [accessed 1 May 2001].

334. Corman, "Use and Uses of a Congressman's Network"; Mary Schneider Laskowski, "The Impact of Electronic Access to Government Information: What Users and Documents Specialists Think," *Journal of Government Information* 27, no. 2 (2000) [this study investigated government documents information specialists and undergradu-

ates in an economics class]; Wen-Hua Ren, "U.S. Government Information Need, Awareness, and Searching: A Study of Small Business Executives," *Journal of Government Information* 26, no. 5 (1999) [81 respondents whose names were taken from a directory of New Jersey small businesses participated in this study].

335. Ricci, "Towards a Systematic Study of Internet-Based Communication."

336. R. Darin Ellis, "Patterns of E-Mail Requests by Users of an Internet-Based Aging-Services Information System," *Family Relations* 48, no. 1 (1999) [this study investigated individuals sending email messages or feedback forms to an aging-services information system].

337. Hwang, "A Comparative Study of Tax-Filing Methods."

338. Bimber, "The Internet and Political Mobilization."

339. Laskowski, "Electronic Access to Government Information."

340. Ren, "U.S. Government Information Need."

341. Corman, "Use and Uses of a Congressman's Network."

342. Ren, "U.S. Government Information Need."

343. Corman, "Use and Uses of a Congressman's Network."

344. Ellis, "Patterns of E-Mail Requests."

345. Ren, "U.S. Government Information Need."

346. Ren, "U.S. Government Information Need."

347. Ellis, "Patterns of E-Mail Requests."

348. Supriya Singh and Annette Ryan, "Gender, Design, and Internet Commerce," *Internet Research: Electronic Networking Applications and Policy* 10, no. 1 (2000) [30 middle-income Australian women who have Internet access at home participated in this research].

349. Hugh Pattinson and Linden Brown, "Chameleons in Marketplace: Industry Transformation in the New Electronic Marketing Environment," *Internet Research: Electronic Networking Applications and Policy* 6, no. 2/3 (1996).

350. United States Federal Trade Commission, Bureau of Consumer Protection, "Online Profiling: A Report to Congress," http://www.ftc.gov/os/2000/06/onlineprofilingreportjune2000.pdf, June 2000 [accessed 1 March 2001].

351. Steven Bellman, Gerald L. Lohse, and Eric J. Johnson, "Predictors of Online Buying Behavior," *Communications of the ACM* 42, no. 12 (1999) [this study examined 10,180 survey responses from Web users from around the world]; Alka Varma Citrin et al., "Adoption of Internet Shopping: The Role of Consumer Innovativeness," *Industrial Management and Data Systems* 100, no. 7 (2000) [403 undergraduates at a large state university participated in this research]; Lawrence Loh

and Yee-Shyuan Ong, "The Adoption of Internet-Based Stock Trading: A Conceptual Framework and Empirical Results," *Journal of Information Technology* 13, no. 2 (1998) [this study examined individuals involved with an online trading system in Singapore]; Ian Phau and Sui Meng Poon, "Factors Influencing the Types of Products and Services Purchased over the Internet," *Internet Research: Electronic Networking Applications and Policy* 10, no. 2 (2000) [broad sample of Singapore citizens; average of participants: 23.4].

352. Eugene H. Fram and Dale B. Grady, "Internet Shoppers: Is There a Surfer Gender Gap?" *Direct Marketing* 59, no. 9 (1997) [this survey examined 254 female respondents]; S. M. Furnell and T. Karweni, "Security Implications of Electronic Commerce: A Survey of Consumers and Businesses," *Internet Research: Electronic Networking Applications and Policy* 9, no. 5 (1999) [this research involved 64 participants].

353. Karen Weber and Wesley S. Roehl, "Profiling People Searching for and Purchasing Travel Products on the World Wide Web," *Journal of Travel Research* 37, no. 3 (1999) [this study examined research from a previously gathered data set].

354. Ann E. Schlosser, Sharon Shavitt, and Alaina Kafner, "Survey of Users' Attitudes toward Internet Advertising," *Journal of Interactive Marketing* 13, no. 3 (1999) [this study examined a nationally representative sample with 1,004 participants nationwide].

355. Pradeep K. Korgaonkar and Lori D. Wolin, "A Multivariate Analysis of Web Usage," *Journal of Advertising Research* 39, no. 2 (1999) [focus group participants were students from a Southeastern university in the United States; questionnaire and interview participants were 420 consumers from a large Southeastern metropolitan area].

356. Singh and Ryan, "Gender, Design, and Internet Commerce."

357. Joseph M. Jones and Leo R. Vijayasarathy, "Internet Consumer Catalog Shopping: Findings from an Exploratory Study and Directions for Future Research," *Internet Research: Electronic Networking Applications and Policy* 8, no. 4 (1998) [51 undergraduates in a business course at a large Midwestern university participated in this study].

358. Phau and Poon, "Factors Influencing Products and Services."

359. Furnell and Karweni, "Security Implications of Electronic Commerce."

360. Fram and Grady, "Internet Shoppers?"

361. Jones and Vijayasarathy, "Internet Consumer Catalog Shopping."

362. Bellman, Lohse, and Johnson, "Predictors of Online Buying Behavior"; Jones and Vijayasarathy, "Internet Consumer Catalog Shopping."

363. Fram and Grady, "Internet Shoppers?"

364. Fram and Grady, "Internet Shoppers?"

365. Jones and Vijayasarathy, "Internet Consumer Catalog Shopping"; Phau and Poon, "Factors Influencing Products and Services."

366. Furnell and Karweni, "Security Implications of Electronic Commerce."

367. Fram and Grady, "Internet Shoppers?"

368. Naveen Donthu and Adriana Garcia, "The Internet Shopper," *Journal of Advertising Research* 39, no. 3 (1999) [790 respondents chosen from a large city telephone directory participated in this research]; Korgaonkar and Wolin, "A Multivariate Analysis."

369. Weber and Roehl, "Profiling People Searching for Travel Products."

370. Korgaonkar and Wolin, "A Multivariate Analysis."

371. Donthu and Garcia, "The Internet Shopper."

372. Korgaonkar and Wolin, "A Multivariate Analysis."

373. Donthu and Garcia, "The Internet Shopper"; Weber and Roehl, "Profiling People Searching for Travel Products."

374. Donthu and Garcia, "The Internet Shopper."

375. Weber and Roehl, "Profiling People Searching for Travel Products."

376. Citrin et al., "Adoption of Internet Shopping."

377. Donthu and Garcia, "The Internet Shopper."

378. Bellman, Lohse, and Johnson, "Predictors of Online Buying Behavior."

379. Korgaonkar and Wolin, "A Multivariate Analysis."

380. Citrin et al., "Adoption of Internet Shopping."

381. Donthu and Garcia, "The Internet Shopper."

382. Korgaonkar and Wolin, "A Multivariate Analysis."

383. Donthu and Garcia, "The Internet Shopper."

384. Bellman, Lohse, and Johnson, "Predictors of Online Buying Behavior."

385. Phau and Poon, "Factors Influencing Products and Services."

386. Loh and Ong, "Adoption of Internet-Based Stock Trading."

387. Jones and Vijayasarathy, "Internet Consumer Catalog Shopping."

388. Loh and Ong, "Adoption of Internet-Based Stock Trading."

389. Furnell and Karweni, "Security Implications of Electronic Commerce."

390. Loh and Ong, "Adoption of Internet-Based Stock Trading."

391. Bellman, Lohse, and Johnson, "Predictors of Online Buying Behavior."

392. Furnell and Karweni, "Security Implications of Electronic Commerce."

393. Korgaonkar and Wolin, "A Multivariate Analysis."

394. Furnell and Karweni, "Security Implications of Electronic Commerce"; Loh and Ong, "Adoption of Internet-Based Stock Trading."

395. Bruce Bimber, "Measuring the Gender Gap on the Internet," *Social Science Quarterly* 81, no. 3 (2000) [this study examined 3,032 adults in the United States]; James Katz and Phillip Aspden, "Motivations for and Barriers to Internet Usage: Results of a National Public Opinion Survey," *Internet Research: Electronic Networking Applications and Policy* 7, no. 3 (1997) [2,500 respondents in a national random telephone sample participated in this research]; Carmen Gomez Mont, "The Social Uses of Internet in Mexico: A Case Study," *Telematics and Informatics* 16, no. 3 (1999); Andrew S. Patrick and Alex Black, "Who Is Going Online? Results from the National Capital FreeNet," *Internet Research: Electronic Networking Applications and Policy* 7, no. 4 (1997) [Patrick and Black investigated 1,073 users of the Capital FreeNet].

396. GVU, "GVU's Tenth WWW User Survey," *GVU User Surveys*, http://www.gvu.gatech.edu/user_surveys/, October 1998 [accessed 22 May 2001] [the GVU researches Internet users]; Clifford Perry, "Travelers on the Internet: A Survey of Internet Users," *Online* 19 (March/April 1995) [84 Internet users participated in this research].

397. Thompson S. H. Teo and Vivien K. Lim, "Gender Differences in Internet Usage and Task Preference," *Behaviour and Information Technology* 19, no. 4 (2000) [Teo investigated Internet users in Singapore]; Thompson S. H. Teo, "Differential Effects of Occupation on Internet Usage," *Internet Research: Electronic Networking Applications and Policy* 8, no. 2 (1998) [1,346 Internet users in Singapore participated in this research].

398. Patrick and Black, "Who Is Going Online?"; Perry, "Travelers on the Internet."

399. Gomez Mont, "The Social Uses of Internet in Mexico."

400. Bimber, "Measuring the Gender Gap on the Internet"; Katz and Aspden, "Motivations for and Barriers to Internet Usage"; Lee

Rainie and Dan Packel, "More Online, Doing More" (Washington, D.C.: Pew Internet and American Life Project, 2001) [this survey investigated a national sample using two surveys ; the first survey had 4,606 participants and the second had 3,493]; Reijo Savolainen, "Embarking on the Internet: What Motivates People?," *ASLIB Proceedings* 52, no. 5 (2000); Reijo Savolainen, "The Role of the Internet in Information Seeking: Putting the Networked Services in Context," *Information Processing and Management* 35, no. 6 (1999) [the two Savolainen studies investigated 23 people living in Finland].

401. Katherine Turner and Margaret Kendall, "Public Use of the Internet at Chester Library," *Information Research* 5, no. 3 (2000) [178 respondents returned questionnaires; nine were interviewed].

402. Kraut et al., "The Home Net Field Trial."

403. Joy Tillotson, Joan Cherry, and Marshall Clinton, "Internet Use through the University of Toronto Library: Demographics, Destinations, and Users' Reactions," *Information Technology and Libraries* 14 (September 1995) [this study had 505 participants].

404. Bimber, "Measuring the Gender Gap on the Internet."

405. Rainie and Packel, "More Online, Doing More."

406. Kraut et al., "The Home Net Field Trial"; Rainie and Packel, "More Online, Doing More."

407. Teo and Lim, "Gender Differences in Internet Usage."

408. Patrick and Black, "Who Is Going Online?"

409. Gomez Mont, "The Social Uses of Internet in Mexico."

410. Turner and Kendall, "Public Use of the Internet at Chester Library."

411. Kraut et al., "The Home Net Field Trial"; Patrick and Black, "Who Is Going Online?"

412. GVU, "GVU's Tenth WWW User Survey"; Katz and Aspden, "Motivations for and Barriers to Internet Usage"; Tillotson, Cherry, and Clinton, "Internet Use through the University of Toronto Library."

413. Gomez Mont, "The Social Uses of Internet in Mexico."

414. Rainie and Packel, "More Online, Doing More."

415. Turner and Kendall, "Public Use of the Internet at Chester Library."

416. GVU, "GVU's Tenth WWW User Survey."

417. Teo, "Differential Effects of Occupation on Internet Usage."

418. Katz and Aspden, "Motivations for and Barriers to Usage."

419. Rainie and Packel, "More Online, Doing More."

420. Kraut et al., "The Home Net Field Trial."

421. Rainie and Packel, "More Online, Doing More."

422. Katz and Aspden, "Motivations for and Barriers to Usage."

423. Patrick and Black, "Who Is Going Online?"

424. GVU, "GVU's Tenth WWW User Survey"; Katz and Aspden, "Motivations for and Barriers to Usage"; Kraut et al., "The Home Net Field Trial."

425. Rainie and Packel, "More Online, Doing More."

426. Katz and Aspden, "Motivations for and Barriers to Usage."

427. Savolainen, "Embarking on the Internet: What Motivates People?"

428. Savolainen, "Embarking on the Internet: What Motivates People?"

429. Katz and Aspden, "Motivations for and Barriers to Internet Usage."

430. Savolainen, "Embarking on the Internet."

431. Kraut et al., "The Home Net Field Trial."

432. Tillotson, Cherry, and Marshall Clinton, "Internet Use through the University of Toronto Library"; Turner and Kendall, "Public Use of the Internet at Chester Library."

433. Perry, "Travelers on the Internet"; Savolainen, "The Role of the Internet in Information Seeking."

434. Rainie and Packel, "More Online, Doing More."

435. Rainie and Packel, "More Online, Doing More."

436. Savolainen, "The Role of the Internet in Information Seeking."

437. Rainie and Packel, "More Online, Doing More."

438. GVU, "GVU's Tenth WWW User Survey."

439. Teo and Lim, "Gender Differences in Internet Usage."

440. Teo and Lim, "Gender Differences in Internet Usage."

441. Kraut et al., "The Home Net Field Trial."

442. Bimber, "Measuring the Gender Gap on the Internet."

443. Rainie and Packel, "More Online, Doing More."

444. Rainie and Packel, "More Online, Doing More."

445. GVU, "GVU's Tenth WWW User Survey."

446. Patrick and Black, "Who Is Going Online?"

447. Teo, "Differential Effects of Occupation on Internet Usage."

448. Rainie and Packel, "More Online, Doing More."

449. Katz and Aspden, "Motivations for and Barriers to Usage."

450. Perry, "Travelers on the Internet."

451. Turner and Kendall, "Public Use of the Internet at Chester Library."

452. Katz and Aspden, "Motivations for and Barriers to Usage."

453. Katz and Aspden, "Motivations for and Barriers to Usage."
454. Savolainen, "The Role of the Internet in Information Seek-ing."

Chapter 5

The User's View of the Internet

The Internet story is a composite of many overlapping and intersecting scenarios. It is the story of a technology innovation that is catalyzing cultural, social, political, and economic transformations on a global scale. It is also the story (in fact, a vast collection of stories) of individual people using the Internet. When a person uses the Internet, his or her understanding and perceptions of the network are enhanced. That individual's construct of the Internet is altered and new elements are added. In effect, the Internet is transformed at this microlevel. Through a composite or collection of these usings, we can also see the trajectories for innovating and developing the network. The Internet has evolved in response to the pressures of the collective usings of people. With tools that are sensitive enough to understand and interpret Internet usings, stakeholders in Internet development will be able to plan for their ongoing involvement with the Internet story. The user's view of the Internet is a first attempt at providing this sort of instrument.

Internet Usings:
Reduction and Amplification

The Internet has form. It is a set of technologies and protocols and standards. It is a set of connections among services and it is the services themselves. The Internet also exists in the minds of people. People perceive it and build representations of it in their minds. People relate to the Internet because it intersects with their lives in the usings, uses, applications, and contexts described in chapter 4. Out of these doings, people build individual constructs of the Internet. In this way, the Internet becomes more than wires, connections, protocols, and services. It is a composite of individual impressions of the impact that using has on the lives and doings of people. It exists in the minds of people in the form of knowledge structures. These constructs allow people to interpret and make sense of things. When we encounter new things we use existing knowledge structures to link the unknown with the known. The Internet has been taking shape in the minds of people in this way over time. The network in form is evolving through innovation. It is also evolving through the using constructs of people—the *user's view* of the Internet.

When we study the phenomenon of the Internet through the lens of using, our attention is drawn to the micromoment of network using by an individual person. Each micromoment of using that we observe advances us one step forward in opposing directions on the continuum that bridges the gap between matter and form (see figure 5.1). This figure is adapted from Latour (see figure 3.2). Each step toward either end of the continuum brings us closer to understanding the object of study through reduction and amplification. Reduction occurs in the form of a more refined understanding of the individual users involved in the micromoment of Internet using, and we move a step at a time toward amplification in the form of a generalized construct of the Internet. In one direction (reduction), we better understand the unique constructs of the Internet occurring for an individual person. At the same time (in the other direction), we are building our understanding of the general qualities of the Internet construct for all people.

In composite, the study of these usings builds our understanding of the phenomenon of the Internet. The overall outcome of this gap bridging is what we are calling the *user's view of the Internet*. The important thing to note is that our construct is always a work in progress. Our observations go on forever with continuous reductions and amplifications resulting from the observation of micromoments of using. In fact, these refinements will continue in the absence of any form of scientific observation. The Internet is highly dynamic in form and so too is the user's view of the Internet. The Internet as a user construct is constantly transforming at the level of the individual through the incremental perceptions of the network which occur with each successive using. It is also being transformed at the amplification end of the continuum (see figure 5.1) because the collective usings of people are setting the agenda for modifying, developing, and evolving the Internet.

Figure 5.1. Constructing the User's View of the Internet

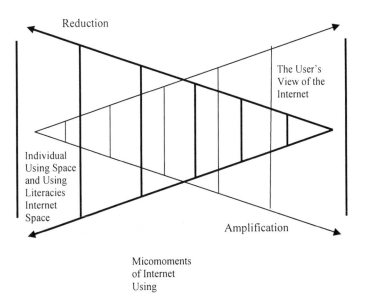

Reduction

The User's
View of the
Internet

Individual
Using Space
and Using
Literacies
Internet
Space

Amplification

Micomoments
of Internet
Using

Usings

The first step in understanding something new is to place it within a familiar context and to use it for a familiar purpose. Technology using follows this pattern. People find the application of new technologies in their world of tasks and doings. How will this application serve a familiar purpose? How will it help me do better the things that I normally do? As a technology becomes more accepted in the daily routines of people, these usings may become more experimental. Some people begin to look for innovative applications. They want to find a using for the technology that is not bending the using to suit the technology but seeing if the technology can be bent to suit the using.

In the early stages of the evolution and development of the Internet, most micromoments of Internet using by people were related to professional tasks (see figure 5.2). ARPANET researchers used fledgling networking technologies to share research data and to communicate with colleagues. Faculty members and researchers at universities who were attached to the NSFNet viewed the Internet as a tool for doing research and teaching. Librarians perceived the Internet in relation to their professional functions of information provision, information searching, information storing, and collection building and augmentation. Teachers developed constructs for the Internet that centered on information transfer, resources, content, and the learning of new things. Legislators and policy makers developed constructs for the Internet that centered on access to constituents, getting their message across, finding efficiencies in the services offered by public utilities, dealing with social and public policy issues such as the digital divide, and universal service. Business professionals and entrepreneurs developed constructs for the Internet as access to markets and commercial enterprise, new conceptions of the chain of production, and opportunities for new product or service development.

Figure 5.2. Professional Tasks and Internet Using

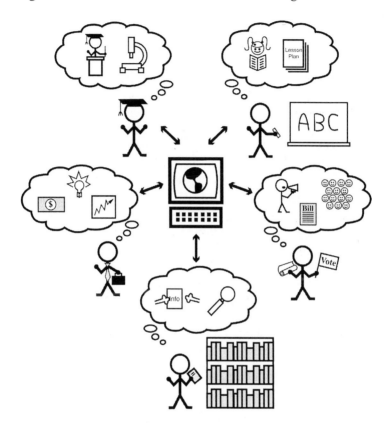

Over time, Internet using in relation to professional roles and workplace tasks has remained the foundation of the user's view of the Internet. The network continues to be constructed (in the user's view) as a tool for facilitating professional action, workplace productivities, efficiency, and competitive advantage. This construct has a number of sources. Obviously, it emerges from the usings of people in the professional setting (people gain their impression of the Internet as a professional tool from these usings), but characteristics of the using can also be prescribed by the professional setting itself. The data presented in chapter 4 make it clear that Internet usings are not always a matter of individual choice. They can also be imposed by an existing workplace infrastructure. The user's view of the Internet can result from imposed as well as self-regulated using.

The using construct that views the Internet as a professional tool can also be defined by the usings of others or assumptions about the value of using types. The professional context assumes that if all professionals were to use the Internet in certain ways then the roles and functions of the profession would be enhanced. The views of individual practitioners of that profession are inevitably influenced by these views and a construct of the Internet emerges. In this case, the source of the construct is not usings at the personal level, but usings at the potential level or perhaps the usings of other practitioners. These usings may be observed personally, or an individual may hear or read about a particular using. An individual may have a personal construct that views the Internet as an environment for research collaboration, for example, without ever having used the network for this purpose. We know that people are mindful of the usings of their professional peers because most users turn to their colleagues when they need instruction on how to use the Internet for a particular purpose. In this case, the individual knows that the colleague or friend has derived benefit from a particular using and they want to try this using themselves. This helping can, in turn, reinforce the using construct.

In recent years, Internet using has entered the home and this has changed the character of many first-time usings of the Internet. For many people, a first-time encounter with the Internet is now occurring in the home rather than at school or work. These first using constructs are often greatly influenced by a parent, guardian, or older sibling who introduces the new user to the Internet. For an adult first-time user, the home using construct can be affected by a partner, spouse, or perhaps a teenage child. In all cases, the construct of the Internet will be based on the using that has motivated the first encounter and the assumed usings that may have motivated the purchase of the Internet connection in the home.

Through Internet usings at home and regular usings of the Internet at work, people are building Internet constructs that give the network intersecting influences in their lives. The constructs of the Internet as a workplace productivity tool are being embellished by these personal usings. People are experimenting with nonwork usings of the Internet and finding that it is a place where they can buy things, play games, and have fun. They can find people who are interested in the same music they like or share the same political or cultural perspectives. These usings are transforming the user's view of the Internet. Everyday usings are expanding the Internet construct from work-based utilitarian to everyday utilitarian—Internet as tool and toy.

Clearly, the user's view of the Internet is a learning construct. Because the Internet is changing and developing so rapidly, many Internet usings involve encounters with new things (services, websites, advertisements, businesses, etc.). The World Wide Web in particular is so interlinked that people encounter new experiences and potential usings while they engage in conventional using behaviors. The Internet using construct for any individual is, therefore, a knowing and doing space that is building and transforming. The user's view of the Internet changes with each micromoment of Internet use. In some cases, changes to a user's construct of the Internet may be visceral. In other cases, the using more overtly alters the way the individual views the Internet. Either way, Internet using reinforces a view for individuals that the Internet is constantly changing and transforming. The user's view of the Internet that emerges from these usings has three components—the using space, using literacies, and Internet space.

Using Space

People manage the uncertainties that accompany the construct of the Internet as constantly changing and transforming by anchoring their perceptions of the network with using realities that have meaning for them. Users establish a space where their using takes place regularly and successfully. This space is the personal and professional using environment of an individual. It is where the individual is expert and he or she can relate Internet using to regular functions in daily professional and personal life. The Internet using space is a component of the information, communication, and recreation horizon of the individual. It is where individuals feel confident and everyday in their using of the Internet. It is where Internet using touches their lives and where the Internet using actually becomes an inherent part of the task, activity, or pastime. In the using space, the individual is not "sending email," he or she is communicating with a friend or colleague; the individual is not "searching the Internet," he or she is making holiday plans, or doing research for a school assignment, or finding out about a utilities bill and so on.

At the using space, the construction of Internet is not of a tangible entity ("The Internet"). The using space is individual and intimate. It is like a sphere of influence—the using horizon. Individuals perceive their own sphere of influence in terms of the people they contact and the resources they can access—the actions they are free to take. There is also a sense in which individuals see a personal impact. The using space relates to this construct of self. Here, the individual can access these resources, use these services, and make contact with these people.

As control over features of Internet using move away from the individual's sphere of influence, the user loses confidence, begins to externalize or depersonalize the processes, and may be reluctant to engage in the using behavior. A good example of where this is happening is online shopping. The key to online purchasing is confidence that the transaction is taking place within the sphere of influence of the individual—the using horizon. When users lack confidence in the security of the transaction, they are really saying that they feel that they lack control at this point in the process. The transaction has moved out of the using space. It is outside the sphere of influence of the individual and may be susceptible to corruption.

Email is a good example of a common using space component. The data appearing in chapter 4 show that email using has become so commonplace that most people have moved this service into their using space. Sending and receiving email does not require a conscious effort. Emailing has become a part of everyday life, professionally and personally.

The Internet using space is a composite of the professional and personal dimensions of the individual. As we have mentioned, the usings that would originally have established the Internet using space for most individuals were professional, but increased access to the Internet has meant that people are now using the Internet in other aspects of their lives. It is possible for the using space to include applications of the Internet that are externally imposed, but these applications must be endorsed by the individual because the using space represents an optimistic view of the Internet. It is within this space that regular and automatic usings occur. The Internet using space, for most people, is a composite of individual (professional and nonwork) constructs of Internet utility.

The Internet using space is nourished by the events of everyday life that require interventions and actions mediated by Internet technologies and services. The using space grows or shrinks like a muscle depending upon how regularly it is used. It is defined and reinforced by those episodes of Internet using that have a positive impact on the life of the individual. Using spaces are unique to individuals. The Internet using space can vary according to attributes of the individual such as personal innovativeness, attitude toward technology adoption, income, profession, access to the Internet, frequency of use, creativity, intelligence, gender, age, and ethnicity.

In the Internet using space, individuals increasingly perceive the Internet utilities of everyday life in a tool or toy construct. The tool construct emerges from the usings that apply the Internet to tasks and perceive the Internet as the mechanism for facilitating these tasks. The construct most logically arises first in the work context and is reinforced here, but it has also infiltrated the nonwork realm where the user sees an application for the Internet as a tool in personal aspects of his or her life. An example of this is the translation of email from a workplace tool into a tool for making contact with friends. As the using space develops for any individual, the translation of the Internet as a tool for enhancing the functions of everyday life—not just professional life—increases.

The construct of the Internet as a toy is more complex. The construct can arise from Internet use at work or home. It is often a next-step using construct. The Internet user is always seeking utility but not always seeking fun in the using space. Often tool usings motivate an individual to consider toy usings. This is not the same as recreational using of the Internet. The Internet can be a tool for recreational purposes. For example, we can use the Internet to locate information about a holiday destination, book flights for a vacation, and so forth. This is the translation of the tool capabilities of the Internet moved from workplace application to recreational pursuits. Toy usings focus on the recreational qualities of the Internet itself. For example, younger users are playing games on the Internet.

With tool usings of the Internet, the outcome is a task. For toy using, the outcome is fun and recreation. Some users (e.g., some teenagers) value the toy usings above the tool usings in their view of the Internet, and others vice versa. The relative dimensions of each in the using space depend on the individual, but generally the research data reveal that people are seeking fun as well as utility from Internet using. For some users, the intuitive qualities of Internet using literacies (discussed next) enhance the toy view of the Internet. For some, it is fun to explore how to use the Internet to achieve the purposes of task completion or recreation.

It could be claimed that tool usings provide a more detailed construction of the Internet for users. The chain of transformations that produce the tool construct include more micromoments of Internet using than are required for the toy construct. People need to be convinced of the utility of the Internet from usings that show value in the form of outcomes. It is perhaps less difficult to convince an individual that something is fun.

The qualities of the Internet using space (size and complexity) depend on many attributes of the individual user, but most people accept a personal limit in terms of Internet expertise. Few people claim to be expert users of the Internet. Most recognize that their using space is a discrete and small sampling of the potential usings of the Internet and that, beyond this space, significant transformations, developments, and growth are taking place in the Internet world. There is an Internet explosion taking place beyond the boundaries of the self. The user's view accommodates this unsettling notion through literacies that link the using space with Internet space. These literacies help the Internet user to accept the limitations of his or her intimate knowledges of the Internet. They help to maneuver the user through Internet space when required.

Using Literacies

The second component of the user's view of the Internet is the set of literacies that individuals acquire and use for their interactions with Internet services. These literacies are the tools of using. They provide the link between the using space (described above) and Internet space (discussed next). In the mind's eye of the user, these are the skills that must be acquired for effective using of the Internet. Where these literacies intersect with the using space, their role is fundamental, automatic, and visceral, so the user's view of the Internet distinguishes these literacies from the using space. They are separate from this space in the user's view because they are the tools that enable the individual to deal with the wider world of Internet space. They are separated from the using space in the user's view of the Internet because the individual user regards these literacies as something that he or she must learn.

These literacies can be acquired intuitively or through individual learning styles or preferences, but Internet users generally acquire the using literacies through self-instruction. At one point in the development of the Internet, these literacies were very complex. They were associated with the specialized skills of particular professional groups. People needed to know arcane commands and computer languages to use Internet services. This appealed to some users and repelled others. As the number of people using the Internet increased, so too did the pressures to make using literacies more intuitive. New-generation Internet users are, therefore, acquiring using literacies in their initial encounters with the Internet or finding that the technology literacies they already have allow them to engage in successful interactions with Internet services. Using literacies are becoming less of a barrier to Internet use for most people. Data from studies identify issues such as access to appropriate technology, connection speeds, and cost as the most significant constraints to Internet using from a user perspective.

The tensions of acquiring using literacies are also diminishing. This is occurring for two reasons. First, the model upon which Internet transformations have been occurring has remained reasonably stable over recent years. The World Wide Web, websites, browsers, search engines, and directories have been around for some years. The growths and transformations that are occurring relate primarily to numbers of users and the size of the Internet, accessibility and interactivity, variety of services, speed, and volumes of data traffic. There have not been correspondingly vast increases in the complexities of Internet using. The using literacies required for using websites and services have remained reasonably stable within this model of development. Second, the tensions of acquiring using literacies have diminished because we are now designing technologies that demand fewer literacies or make use of existing models of use. For example, many general-purpose software applications (e.g., word processing, publishing, database, and spreadsheet) have incorporated Internet-enabling functions that extend the uses of this software into the Internet environment. If we know how to produce a document in a word processor, for example, we can format that same document as a Web page. The literacies associated with using everyday technology tools are, therefore, beginning to intersect with Internet using literacies.

With this said, it is important not to understate how essential using literacies are to the user's view of the Internet. These literacies, from the user's point of view, link the individual to the wider Internet. They are the methods and tools the individual uses to test assumptions about the utility of the Internet space. They allow the user to accommodate the hyperbole of Internet growth and development—to see if the Internet can indeed serve projected purposes in daily professional and personal life. Using literacies provide the individual with confidence that even though they have no control over the scope and scale of the Internet, they can enter this space, navigate these services, and exit unharmed.

Herein lies the distinction between using literacies for the user's view of the Internet and information and technology literacies in general. The information field has been stressing for many years the fundamental importance of information skills and technology literacies. These key skills are being reinforced in schools and colleges as the living skills of the information age. They are defined in such a way that a professional (for example, a librarian) can judge the success of a user's information searching. It is surprising when these professionals note that, although an information search is clearly by their standards unsuccessful, a user might still claim that he or she is satisfied with this using of the Internet. The reason for this is that the individual is applying the standards of his or her using literacies to the Internet interaction (the user's view of the Internet) rather than the information or technology literacy standards of the professional. In other words, Internet using literacies in the user's view of the Internet belong to the individual and serve, for that individual, the purposes already described.

The using literacies component of the user's view of the Internet is somewhat analogous to the relationship between a car and driving skills. Most people drive cars with very limited knowledge of the internal combustion engine and the electronic systems that make it work. Similarly, most users are not interested in the technological dimensions of the Internet. They don't need to know the technological components of the Internet to make it work. Instead, people need the literacies to make the services of the Internet function in relation to the uses that they are pursuing. Clearly, using literacies are enhanced by individual experiences, practice, and the example or instruction of others. As an individual's using literacies develop, his or her perception of the Internet space also changes and develops.

Internet Space

The final component of the user's view of the Internet is Internet space. Users have conceptions of some "wide blue yonder"—the open landscape of the Internet that exists beyond the using space and is beyond any individual's control. Internet space is outside the individual and it includes perceptions of the Internet that arise from the views of others as well as personal experience. It is a space filled with assertions about the values and qualities that arise from and are tested by firsthand and secondhand usings. It is big, dynamic, and challenging.

Internet space is where the fears and negative perceptions of the user's view of the Internet reside and are tested. It can be filled with uncertainty when an individual's using literacies are limited or other more significant constraints such as cost, access, and speed affect the individual's Internet using. These perceptions and constraints can limit or hamper the Internet using that will confirm or disconfirm the qualities of Internet space for the individual.

On the whole, however, Internet space from the user's view of the Internet is optimistic and positive. It is heavily influenced by hyperbole, the positive opinions of others, and the untested but upbeat views of the individual. Until proven otherwise, users will perceive Internet space as a source for the information, people, services, and processes they require ("I could find that on the Internet"; "I know it's out there somewhere"). When the individual applies his or her using literacies to test this assumed utility by interacting with Internet space, the construct of Internet space will be altered by this using. If the process is successful, then the Internet construct will include this form of using. If the outcomes of the process are of high value and become common practice, then this using may be placed in the using space and become part of this more intimate perception of the Internet.

In the Internet space, perceptions and expressions of the network construct it as a tangible thing. Overall, this is a construct of The Internet as a place. Users indicate that they are *on* the Internet or they will *visit* a website. Using in the Internet space is centered on this construction of moving or maneuvering around a place. The Internet space exists beyond the individual's notion of self and orbit of influence. In order to bring this entity into a relationship with the self, the user's view of the Internet creates constructs of familiar entities and perceives the Internet as analogous to these conceptions. In the user's view of the Internet, Internet space may be analogous to a library or an encyclopedia or a brain or an information superhighway (see figure 5.3). Clearly, the hyperbole and rhetoric surrounding the evolution of the network has contributed to, and exploited, this component of the user's view of the Internet.

These constructs mean that an individual can enter Internet space doing familiar things like browsing, reading, window shopping, buying, searching, or chatting. The Internet becomes less threatening and more personal. In fact, Internet space is about finding the connection with self (through using), and more often than not this link is based on positive associations. The constructs that ultimately motivate an Internet use are obviously more likely to be positive than negative. People are attempting to build a closer relationship with the Internet. The ultimate test of these constructs is Internet using by the individual. Usings will confirm or alter the individual's perception of Internet space. They may confirm a positive construct of information close at hand. They may also establish negative using constructs such as getting lost in Internet space or not being able to find things again or being frustrated by having to sift through an overwhelming volume of retrieved information.

Personal usings and perceptions are not the only basis for views of Internet space. As indicated previously, public perceptions and the views of colleagues, peers, friends, and members of the family can influence this aspect of the user's view of the

Figure 5.3: Conceptions of Internet Space

Internet. In fact, a person who has never used the Internet will nonetheless have a view of Internet space. Such an individual would have no using space and few using literacies, but an Internet nonuser will still have a perception of Internet space. This perception is constructed out of the using views of others. In describing the Internet to a nonuser, individuals normally resort to communicating particular versions of Internet space. A teenager, for example, might use conceptions of Internet space as a universe of knowledge to convince a parent that access to the Internet is worthwhile. Nonusers become users of the Internet because the version of Internet space that has been conveyed to them by others through personal contact, the media, or colleagues is so compelling that they now seek proof of concept through using. Use will be advanced by using literacies and may also ultimately result in the development of the using space.

Figure 5.4. The User's View of the Internet

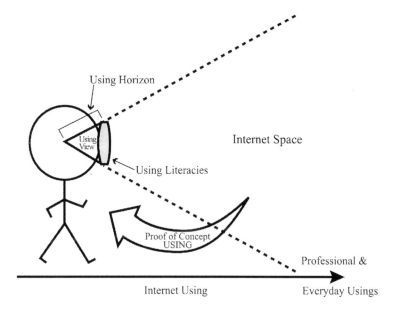

The User's View of the Internet

In summary, the user's view of the Internet is a construct of do-ings, behavings, spaces, processes, people, and things that form the using space, using literacies and Internet space of an individual. The user's view of the Internet is an explication of the fol-lowing principles (see figure 5.4):

1. *Internet using is proof of concept.*
       People construct the Internet through using (their own using or the usings of others). Usings elaborate and en-

hance the user's view of the Internet. Each micromoment
of Internet using is a learning moment. When we have
proof of concept through Internet using, the construct of
the Internet enters the using space of the individual and
is absorbed, adopted, and diffused into the everyday usings and behavings of the individual. Individuals are
masters of their Internet using space.

2. *Internet using occurs in contexts.*

When people use the Internet, they see this as part of the
professional task or the recreational activity that they are
involved in. Within the using space of the individual,
constructs of the Internet are not about answering the
question, *What is the Internet?* They are about how
Internet using fits with and facilitates what I want to or
need to do.

3. *Fun, utility, and frequency of using build the using space.*

People seek application and translation from their Internet using. Internet using is fundamentally about finding
purpose, fun, efficiency, productivity, and outcome.
Tool and toy constructs motivate the micromoments of
Internet using. The tool construct is possibly more powerful for giving rise to subsequent usings on a regular
basis, but a combination of the two is important. The
user brings to each micromoment of Internet using expectations of utility and value, fun, committed time, and
expense. The using space can grow or shrink. If components of the using space are not used regularly, these un-
derused elements may disappear. Frequency of using is
critical to building the properties of the using space.

4. *People explore and monitor Internet space with using litera-*
   cies.

Using literacies bring the Internet space closer to the using space. Using literacies give people confidence to
visit Internet space. Users regard these literacies as tools

for contact but not for control or deep-level understanding. Even regular users rarely claim to be Internet experts.

5. *Internet space does not require proof of concept and can be heavily influenced by the perceptions and usings of others.*

    The user's view of the Internet deals with the tensions of a space beyond individual control through simplistic conceptualizations or constructs that associate Internet space with familiar entities. These are unique to individuals but may be based on the usings and perceptions of others. It is possible for individuals to have a view of the Internet without ever having used the network.

6. *The user's view of the Internet is upbeat and optimistic.*

    People want to find the Internet experience positive. The new-user view of the Internet is heavily influenced by positive perceptions built out of the rhetoric and hyperbole that surround the Internet. As an individual builds the using space from his or her using experiences (micromoments of Internet using), the components of the using space are the positive, useful, fun aspects of the Internet for that individual.

A Note to Internet Stakeholders

Throughout this book, there has been reference made to Internet stakeholders. Who are the people that have some share or role in the use and development of the Internet? Many readers will recognize themselves as Internet stakeholders as they see themselves in the construct of the user's view of the Internet. Internet stakeholders are people who use and will use the Internet to engage in professional tasks. At one level we see a set of stakeholders who are developing or producing services, resources, products, or entities that occupy the Internet space. There are also stakeholders who have incorporated the Internet fundamentally into professional actions. The Internet in this case is the medium for professional practice. There are also stakeholders who engage in professional activities and practices that rely on effective Internet use and exploit the tools, resources, services, and innovations of the Internet. In this case, professional tasks are completed using Internet services. The Internet is a productivity tool, as opposed to an agent for professional role transformation. Finally we have stakeholders who are general-purpose users of the Internet. The network is not a fundamental component of professional practice for them, but Internet using has insinuated itself into their everyday life. These stakeholders look for information on the Internet, communicate with people using the Internet, and shop and have fun using Internet services.

To sum up, Internet stakeholders are:

- Developers who are building components for Internet space
- Professionals who use the Internet in fundamental (transformational) ways to practice their profession
- Professionals who do familiar professional tasks with Internet tools
- People who use the Internet for the tasks and pleasures of everyday life

Listing these stakeholder classes makes it clear that all people who use the Internet are in one way or another affected by its evolution and transformations. All the stakeholders above are also users of the Internet, and in this way, the model presented as the user's view of the Internet belongs to the constituents of each stakeholder category. Many people belong to more than one stakeholder category. As an Internet user, the reader of this book should see himself or herself in the construct of using space, using literacies, and Internet space. It is a construct for individuals. It is also a construct that recommends some attention by those who will most directly influence the future of the Internet. These are the stakeholders at the top of the list above—the developers and professionals who are building or using the Internet in transformational ways. As we have seen from the Internet story to date, however, the groundswell of Internet using by all stake-holders from the everyday to the high-end user feeds an impetus for Internet evolution (using trajectories for innovation) and this in itself draws attention to the importance of a clearer under-standing the user's view of the Internet.

The construct of using space is of critical importance to the Internet developer and the professional who is using the Internet as a medium for professional action. Developers might be creat-ing new Internet sites or services, or ways of offering service or transacting business on the Internet. They may be those who are creating new technologies or functionalities for the Internet. Those who use the Internet for professional action catalyze the Internet usings of others or engage professional actions across the medium of the Internet. Here, we include professionals such as librarians and educators (at all levels), researchers and jour-nalists, public policy advocates, marketing professionals, Inter-net business or e-commerce professionals, and others. For this group of stakeholders, the user's view of the Internet recom-mends professional actions and developmental innovations that intersect as much as possible with the using space of customers, colleagues, students, and constituencies.

This is true in particular for e-commerce developers. The reluctance of many users to engage in online shopping because they are concerned by the security and privacy of transactions highlights the importance of shifting e-commerce into the using space of the shopper. Reluctant online shoppers perceive online commercial transactions as occurring in Internet space—in a space beyond their control. Users need to perceive these transac-tions as occurring within their using horizon—equivalent to those at their corner store or in their mall where they know who they are doing business with, who is taking their money, and the quality of the goods that they are buying. These confidences come with positive experiences. Proof of concept and frequency of use will move the online shopping experience out of the Inter-net space and into the using space of the individual, where the user perception is not that he or she is using the Internet but that he or she is obtaining goods that are needed in the most convenient and enjoyable way.

Efforts to create these more intimate, individual relationships between the online shopper and vendor are under way. The building of customer profiles based on previous purchases is one example. The use of online shopping carts and the ability to browse and search for desired products are further examples. The point at which the shopper enters the phase of exchanging money is the critical moment of intimacy and trust. The shopper needs to know that this moment of Internet using is private and secure—that the micromoment of using is occurring in his or her own using space. It is vital that the transfer of money is perceived as taking place within a customer-controlled rather than vendor-controlled context.

Educators should also be mindful of the using space of the user's view of the Internet. Teachers should attempt to energize pedagogies within the Internet using space of learners. The integration of Internet using with the curriculum is certainly a part of this. But more than integration with content, the user's view of the Internet suggests that the student must perceive Internet using as part of learning—not as an extra challenge to learning new content. The intention is to move the learner to the intimate, individualized level of technology acceptance and utilization that occurs in the using space.

There are some steps that must be taken to move the learner toward automatic, even unconscious, Internet usings that facilitate learning. Clearly, the Internet must be readily accessible and used frequently in a wide variety of ways in the school, college, or university setting. The student should turn automatically to Internet tools and services to support various forms of learning, communication, and problem solving. Internet using should be second nature so that the focus for the student is on learning rather than the novelty or difficulties of an Internet technology or service. Using literacies are obviously a crucial factor. Educators can see from the user's view of the Internet that although these literacies may be taught, they are also unique points of reference for an individual. Teachers may interpret the general quality of these literacies in students, but must acknowledge, at the individual level, that students will construct for themselves the dimensions and characteristics of Internet space according to the level of confidence they have in their own using literacies. Enhancing this confidence with learning experiences that reinforce individual, meaningful engagements with the Internet is vital.

Using literacies are also an important feature of the user's view of the Internet for developers. Using literacies are the sensemaking, translating, and maneuvering techniques that a person will bring to engagements with the Internet space. People transpose these literacies across micromoments of Internet using. Individuals who learn to access something they need, or do something using a particular method, invariably duplicate that method when the need arises for a similar type of Internet using. Minimizing the number and complexity of using literacies that are required to access a new site or use a new service is an important step toward facilitating initial and continuing use. Individuals will also attempt to learn new usings of the Internet on their own. To do this, they attempt to intuitively link their existing literacies with new usings. Internet developers should therefore incorporate, as much as possible, innovations that require common literacies or can be learned from the intuitions or translations of common models of using. The aim of Internet development should be to make Internet using literacies fewer or less complex. Adapting innovations to existing literacies is one way to achieve this.

The user's view of the Internet emphasizes the importance of the qualities of utility and fun. If the Internet is both useful and recreational, using will occur. For those engaged in Internet development or producing new Internet services, the aim should be to find and promote these qualities of the innovation. How does a proposed new service, for example, make it more fun to perform a particular task? How does it make a person more productive and efficient? In what way is the proposed innovation a tool or a toy? Teachers can also exploit this quality of the user's view of the Internet. Fun catalyzes learning. Where the learner finds fun, new knowledges are acquired almost unconsciously.

The choosing of Internet applications that reinforce the fun and the utility of the Internet using for the learner is important.

Finally, for librarians and information professionals, there are several noteworthy features of the user's view of the Internet. Modern information specialists are fundamentally concerned with information provision at the point of need. The Internet is clearly (in terms of using space, using literacies, and Internet space) perceived as the primary tool and medium for information transfer in modern society. In the using space, people unconsciously turn to their desktops to locate the information they need to effectively engage in workplace tasks and everyday activities. In this using space, there is little or no attention given to the values and professional actions that have facilitated the transfer of the needed information to the desktop. In the using space, individuals do not think about knowledge organization, representation, and classification. They do not consider the selection and evaluation of content and its restructuring and packaging. They do not think of the library.

In fact, in the using space of the individual, we find expression of the view that we no longer need libraries. What is the purpose of a library when I can obtain all the information that I need without having to visit one? In the automatic and everyday world of the using space, where the tools of everyday information gathering are immediately at hand, the associations of visiting a library for information or for reference services can seem an extreme inconvenience. The library and information-based interventions that have occurred in order to move needed information to the desktop must be advocated and promoted by the librarian and information specialist so that these perceptions find expression and are valued in the using space. Seamless service does not have to equate with being invisible and unacknowledged.

In the linking space of using literacies and in the Internet space, this is not so much a problem. The frustrations of the Internet space are frequently expressed in the user's view of the Internet as information challenges. Internet space is where information overload occurs, where people find too much information, where people become lost on an information trail, where people lose or misplace information they have found, where people are concerned about the credibility of the information that they locate. There is a view that is reinforced by these perceptions that traditional library know-how is needed to solve the *what-is-out-there* and *how-do-I-find-it* problems of the Internet space. The user's view of the Internet draws attention to the information challenges that people encounter as they use the Internet. It is not enough to connect people with information. People need to be able to evaluate, synthesize, reformulate and restructure, present, and utilize the information they find. Internet using can connect people with information, but this does not necessarily ensure effective information using. The library and information specialist has a role to play in the chain of events that are information processing mediated by Internet using—from information need to information utilization. The information challenges that are highlighted in the Internet space of the user's view of the Internet draw attention to the importance and value of many of the long-standing practices of librarians and information specialists and should provide the context for aggressive advocacy of the major contribution that the information field can make to the future development of the Internet.

The library and information field has a long-standing concern with the information and technology literacies that people need to connect with the information that they require. The information professions have been working for years to define these skills and to offer instructional and support services that help library patrons, people working in organizations, and school and university students and faculty to use information and information technology effectively. These information literacies overlap with the using literacies of the user's view of the Internet. For this reason, we have seen library and information professionals over the last decade taking a role in Internet using literacy instruction, particularly in schools and on university campuses.

The user's view of the Internet provides both a support for this role and a cautionary note. The using literacies of the user's view of the Internet are the individual user's repertoire of methods, skills, and techniques that facilitate meaningful interactions with the Internet. In many respects, they are the personal knowledge structures that individuals bring to the self-learning, sensemaking, and using intuitions that occur in Internet space and also in the using space of the user's view of the Internet. It has become increasingly apparent that people prefer to adapt these literacies and intuitions to their Internet using rather than to seek formal instruction. So, while there are generic literacies that are essential for effective use of information and information technology, it is the distinctive adaptations and applications of these literacies that comprise the automatic and everyday uses of the Internet which occur in the using space of the individual. Information professionals must value these personal versions of using literacy. Evidence that they exist has appeared in many research contexts, where people have declared that they are satisfied with information processes, systems, and services that are clearly, by expert standards, faulty or deficient. The perceptions of users are highly personalized and take account of factors beyond the generic standards set by professionals. Internet usings are a further demonstration of the complex and individual nature of the information doings and behavings of people that continue to intrigue and challenge the information field.

Readers who are interested in the development of the Internet should not consider these few observations to be a complete listing of the ramifications of the user's view of the Internet. The goal here has been to show that a story of Internet transformation and development is being told through the usings of people and that the theoretical construct emerging from the observation of these usings (the user's view of the Internet) can equip the Internet stakeholder with the sensitivities required to reflect on and interpret what these usings are saying about the perceptions of people. Individual stakeholders will make their own interpretations about how these perceptions intersect with and impact upon their particular interest in the Internet. The user's view of the Internet is a lens for continued observing and interpreting and reacting. It should stimulate those who are interested in the story of the Internet to observe and make sense of this ongoing narrative.

Conclusion

The user's view of the Internet provides us with a construct for engagement with individual perceptions of Internet use and the general characteristics of how people perceive the role that the Internet is playing in their professional and everyday living. The formulations of a using space, using literacies, and Internet space that comprise the user's view of the Internet allow us to deconstruct and elaborate how the perceptions of people using the Internet can inform those who are fashioning the future forms of network service and use. Understanding how and why people are using the Internet and how they perceive the Internet through using is vitally important as we anticipate and observe the next generation of Internet development. The phenomenon of the Internet will continue to play a fundamental role in the information and communication dimensions of living in our modern times, but the phenomenon itself will transform and transition through uses and using. We will continue to want to describe and understand the Internet, and over time it will continue to manifest its importance in anticipated and unanticipated ways through the usings of people. Understanding more fully the nature of these usings will give us some insight into what might happen next, because micromoments of Internet using are building the Internet future, but more importantly the user's view of the Internet helps us to support what is happening now.

The user's view of the Internet is a work in progress. It will always be incomplete and unfolding. With each micromoment of Internet using we take a step closer to the reductions and amplifications that bring us insight into the phenomenon that is the Internet. We are one step further on our journey of continuing discovery. The user's view of the Internet tells us how to observe each step and gives insight into where that step might take us, but the composite of the micromoments of using that are building future manifestations of the phenomenon that is the Internet lie in our future. With these micromoments of using the story of the Internet is told. We will observe and wonder.

Bibliography

Abbate, Janet. *Inventing the Internet, Inside Technology.* Cambridge, Mass.: MIT Press, 1999.

Abdoulaye, Kaba, and Shaheen Majid. "Use of the Internet for Reference Services in Malaysian Academic Libraries." *Online Information Review* 24, no. 5 (2000): 381-88.

Abels, Eileen G., Peter Liebscher, and Daniel W. Denman. "Factors That Influence the Use of Electronic Networks by Science and Engineering Faculty at Small Institutions, Part I: Queries." *Journal of the American Society for Information Science* 47, no. 2 (1996): 146-58.

Agarwal, Ritu, and Jayesh Prasad. "Are Individual Differences Germane to the Acceptance of New Information Technologies?" *Decision Sciences* 30, no. 2 (1999): 361-91.

————. "A Conceptual and Operational Definition of Personal Innovativeness in the Domain of Information Technology." *Information Systems Research* 9, no. 2 (1998): 204-15.

Ajzen, Icek. "The Theory of Planned Behavior." *Organizational Behavior and Human Decision Processes* 50 (1991): 179-211.

Ajzen, Icek, and Martin Fishbein. *Understanding Attitudes and Predicting Social Behavior.* Englewood Cliffs, N.J.: Prentice-Hall, 1980.

Alange, Sverker, Staffan Jacobsson, and Annika Jarnehammar. "Some Aspects of an Analytical Framework for Studying the Diffusion of Organizational Innovations." *Technology Analysis & Strategic Management* 10, no. 1 (1998): 3-21.

Allen, Bryce. *Information Tasks: Toward a User-Centered Approach to Information Systems.* San Diego: Academic Press, 1996.

Allen, Kathleen R. *Growing and Managing an Entrepreneurial Business.* Boston: Houghton Mifflin, 1999.

American Psychological Association. Work Group of the American Psychological Association's Board of Educational Affairs (BEA). "Learner-Centered Psychological Principles: A Framework for School Redesign and Reform," http://www.apa.org/ed/lcp.html, 1997 [accessed 5 July 2001].

Anandarajan, Murugan, Claire Simmers, and Magid Igbaria. "An Exploratory Investigation of the Antecedents and Impact of Internet Usage: An Individual Perspective." *Behaviour and Information Technology* 19, no. 1 (2000): 69-85.

Applebee, Andrelyn, Harry Bruce, Peter Clayton, Celina Pascoe, and Edna Sharpe. *Academics Online: A Nationwide Quantitative Study of Australian Academic Use of the Internet.* Adelaide, Australia: Auslib Press, 1998.

Applebee, Andrelyn C., Peter Clayton, and Celina Pascoe. "Australian Academic Use of the Internet." *Internet Research: Electronic Networking Applications and Policy* 7, no. 2 (1997): 85-94.

Arms, C. "A New Information Infrastructure." *Online* 14, no. 5 (1990): 15-22.

Arnold, Stephen E. *Publishing on the Internet: A New Medium for a New Millennium.* Calne, England: Infonortics, 1996.

Association of College and Research Libraries. *Continuity and Transformation: The Promise of Confluence: Proceedings of the Seventh National Conference of the Association of College and Research Libraries, Pittsburgh, Pennsylvania, March 29-April 1, 1995.* Chicago: Association of College and Research Libraries, 1995.

Badham, Richard, and Pelle Ehn. "Tinkering with Technology: Human Factors, Work Redesign, and Professionals in Workplace Innovation." *Human Factors and Ergonomics in Manufacturing* 10, no. 1 (2000): 61-82.

Bane, Adele F., and William D. Milheim. "Internet Insights: How Academics Are Using the Internet." *Computers in Libraries* 15, no. 2 (1995): 32-26.

Bao, Xue-Ming. "Challenges and Opportunities: A Report of the 1998 Library Survey of Internet Users at Seton Hall University." *College and Research Libraries* 59, no. 6 (1998): 535-43.

Barbuto, D. M., and E. E. Cevallos. "End-User Searching: Program Review and Future Prospects." *Reference Quarterly* 31, no. 2 (1991): 214-27.

Beales, Howard, Mike Mazis, Steve Salop, and Richard Staelin. "Consumer Search and Public Policy." *Journal of Consumer Research* 8 (1981): 11-21.

Becker, Henry Jay. "Internet Use by Teachers: Conditions of Professional Use and Teacher-Directed Student Use." Irvine, Calif.: Center for Research on Information Technology and Organizations, 1999.

Becker, Henry Jay, and Jason Ravitz. "The Influence of Computer and Internet Use on Teachers' Pedagogical Practices and Perceptions." *Journal of Research on Computing in Education* 31, no. 4 (1999): 356-85.

Belkin, Nicholas J. "Cognitive Models and Information Transfer." *Social Science Information Studies* 4 (1984): 111-29.

———. "The Cognitive Viewpoint in Information Science." *Journal of Information Science* 16 (1990): 11-15.

Belkin, Nicholas J., C. L. Borgman, H. M. Brooks, T. Bylander, W. B. Croft, P. Daniels, S. Deerwester, E. A. Fox, P. Ingwersen, R. Rada, K. Sparck Jones, R. Thompson, and D. Walker. "Distributed Expert-Based Information Systems: An Interdisciplinary Approach." *Information Processing and Management* 23, no. 5 (1987): 395-409.

Belkin, Nicholas J., T. Seeger, and G. Wersig. "Distributed Expert Problem Treatment as a Model for Information System Analysis and Design." *Journal of Information Science* 5 (1983): 153-67.

Belkin, Nicholas J., and A. Vickery. *Interaction in Information Systems: A Review of Research from Document Retrieval to Knowledge-Based Systems.* Library and Information Research Report 35. London: British Library, 1985.

Bellman, Steven, Gerald L. Lohse, and Eric J. Johnson. "Predictors of Online Buying Behavior." *Communications of the ACM* 42, no. 12 (1999): 32-38.

Benson, Allen C. *The Complete Internet Companion for Librarians.* New York: Neal-Schuman, 1995.

Bertot, John Carlo, Charles R. McClure, William E. Moen, and Jeffrey Rubin. "Web Usage Statistics: Measurement Issues and Analytical Techniques." *Government Information Quarterly* 14, no. 4 (1997): 373-95.

Bidwell, Pam. "In Search of Quality: The Tools and Techniques of Health Researchers on the Internet." *LASIE* 31, no. 3 (2000): 30-41.

Bilal, Dania. "Children's Use of the Yahooligans! Web Search Engine," Part 1, "Cognitive, Physical, and Affective Behaviors on Fact-Based Search Tasks. " *Journal of the American Society for Information Science* 51, no. 7 (2000): 646-65.

Bimber, Bruce. "The Internet and Political Mobilization: Research Note on the 1996 Election Season." *Social Science Computer Review* 16, no. 4 (1998): 391-401.

———. "Measuring the Gender Gap on the Internet." *Social Science Quarterly* 81, no. 3 (2000): 868-76.

Bishop, Ann Peterson. "The Role of Computer Networks in Aerospace Engineering." *Library Trends* 42, no. 4 (1994): 694-729.

Blair, Kristine, and Pamela Takayoshi. *Feminist Cyberscapes: Mapping Gendered Academic Spaces.* Stamford, Conn.: Ablex Publishing, 1999.

Blumberg, Phyllis, and JoAnne Sparks. "Tracing the Evolution of Critical Evaluation Skills in Students' Use of the Internet." *Bulletin of the Medical Library Association* 87, no. 2 (1999): 200-205.

Bonk, Curtis Jay, and Donald J. Cunningham. "Searching for Learner-Centered, Constructivist, and Sociocultural Components of Collaborative Educational Learning Tools." In *Electronic Collaborators: Learner-Centered Technologies for Literacy, Apprenticeship, and Discourse*, edited by Curtis Jay Bonk and Kira S. King, 25-50. Mahwah, N.J.: L. Erlbaum Associates, 1998.

Bonk, Curtis Jay, and Thomas H. Reynolds. "Learner-Centered Web Instruction for Higher-Order Thinking, Teamwork, and Apprenticeship." In *Web-Based Instruction*, edited by Badrul Huda Khan, 167-78. Englewood Cliffs, N.J.: Educational Technology Publications, 1997.

Borchert, Mark. "The Challenges of Cyberspace: Internet Access and Persons with Disabilities." In *Cyberghetto or Cybertopia? Race, Class, and Gender on the Internet*, edited by Bosah L. Ebo, 49-63. Westport, Conn.: Praeger, 1998.

Borgman, Christine L., Donald Owen Case, and Charles T. Meadow. "The Design and Evaluation of a Front-End User Interface for Energy Researchers." *Journal of the American Society for Information Science* 40, no. 2 (1989): 99-109.

———. "Incorporating Users' Information Seeking Styles into the Design of an Information Retrieval Interface." Paper presented at the 48th Annual Meeting of the American Society for Information Science, 1985.

Bronoel, Marie. "The Digital Divide." Seattle: University of Washington, 2000.

Brown, Ann L., and Annemarie S. Palincsar. "Guided, Cooperative Learning and Individual Knowledge Acquisition." In *Cognition and Instruction: Issues and Agendas*, edited by L. Resnick, 393-451. Hillsdale, N.J.: Lawrence Erlbaum Associates, 1989.

Brown, M. E. "A General Model of Information-Seeking Behavior." Paper presented at the 54th Annual Meeting of the American Society for Information Science, 1991.

Bruce, Harry. "A Cognitive View of the Situational Dynamism of User-Centered Relevance Estimation." *Journal of the American Society for Information Science* 45, no. 3 (1994): 142-48.

————. *Internet, AARNet, and Academic Work: A Longitudinal Study.* Canberra, Australia: Australian Government Publication Service, 1996.

————. "Perceptions of the Internet: What People Think of When They Search the Internet for Information." *Internet Research: Electronic Networking Applications and Policy* 9, no. 3 (1999): 187-99.

————. "User Satisfaction with Information Seeking on the Internet." *Journal of the American Society for Information Science* 49, no. 6 (1998): 541-56.

Bruce, Harry, and Peter Clayton. "An Internet Role for the Academic Librarian?" *Australian Academic and Research Libraries* 30, no. 3 (1999): 171-87.

Bruce, Harry, and R. Todd. "Cultural Dimensions of the Reference Service: Is There Unity in Diversity?" Paper presented at the RAISS National Conference, Darwin, Australia, 1993.

Budd, John M. "User-Centered Thinking: Lessons from Reader-Centered Theory." *Reference Quarterly* 34, no. 4 (1995): 487-96.

Budd, John M., and Lynn Silipigni Connaway. "University Faculty and Networked Information: Results of a Survey." *Journal of the American Society for Information Science* 48, no. 9 (1997): 843-52.

Burke, Lynn. "The Tangled Web of E-Voting." *Wired.com.* http://wired.com/news/print/0,1294,37050,00.htm, 26 June 2000 [accessed 1 May 2001].

Busselle, Rick, Joey Reagan, Bruce Pinkleton, and Kim Jackson. "Factors Affecting Internet Use in a Saturated-Access Population." *Telematics and Informatics* 16, nos. 1-2 (1999): 45-58.

Bynum, Terrell Ward, James H. Moor, and American Philosophical Association Committee on Philosophy and Computers. *The Digital Phoenix: How Computers Are Changing Philosophy.* Oxford: Blackwell Publishers, 1998.

Carrier, Rebecca. "On the Electronic Information Frontier: Training the Information-Poor in an Age of Unequal Access." In *Cyberghetto or Cybertopia? Race, Class, and Gender on the Internet,* edited by Bosah L. Ebo, 154-68. Westport, Conn.: Praeger, 1998.

Cerf, Vinton G. "A Brief History of the Internet and Related Networks," *Internet Society.* http://www.isoc.org/internet-history/cerf.html, 2000 [accessed 17 March 2000].

———. "On National Information Infrastructure." *Bulletin of the American Society for Information Science* 20, no. 2 (1994): 24-25.

———. "Some Possible Government Roles in Information Infrastructure." *Serials Review* 21, no. 1 (1995): 11-16.

CERN (European Organization for Nuclear Research). "An Overview of the World Wide Web: History and Growth." http://public.web.cern.ch/Public/ACHIEVEMENTS/WEB/history.html, 3 December 1997 [accessed 12 June 2001].

Chang-Wells, G. M., and G. Wells. "Dynamics of Discourse: Literacy and the Construction of Knowledge." In *Contexts for Learning: Sociocultural Dynamics in Children's Development*, edited by Ellice A. Forman, Norris Minick, and C. Addison Stone, 58-90. New York: Oxford University Press, 1993.

Chase, Larry. *Essential Business Tactics for the Net.* New York: Wiley, 1998.

Chen, Hsinchun, and Vasant Dhar. "Cognitive Process as a Basis for Intelligent Retrieval Systems Design." *Information Processing and Management* 27, no. 5 (1991): 405-32.

Chen, Hsinchun, Andrea L. Houston, Robin R. Sewell, and Bruce R. Schatz. "Internet Browsing and Searching: User Evaluations of Category Map and Concept Space Techniques." *Journal of the American Society for Information Science* 49, no. 7 (1998): 582-603.

Cherny, Lynn. *Conversation and Community: Chat in a Virtual World.* CSLI Lecture Notes, No. 94. Stanford, Calif.: CSLI Publications, 1999.

Chisenga, Justin. "A Study of the Use of the Internet among Library Professionals in Sub-Saharan Africa." *Internet Reference Services Quarterly* 4, no. 1 (1999): 37-50.

Chou, Chien, and Ming-Chun Hsiao. "Internet Addiction, Usage, Gratification, and Pleasure Experience: The Taiwan College Students' Case." *Computers and Education* 35 (2000): 65-80.

Ciolek, T. Matthew. "The Scholarly Uses of the Internet: 1998 Online Survey," *Asia Web Watch: A Register of Statistical Data.* http://www.ciolek.com/PAPERS/InternetSurvey-98.html,15 March 1998 [accessed 27 July 2001].

Citrin, Alka Varma, David E. Sprott, Steven N. Silverman, and Donald E. Stem, Jr. "Adoption of Internet Shopping: The Role of Consumer Innovativeness." *Industrial Management and Data Systems* 100, no. 7 (2000): 294-300.

Clark, Jim, and Owen Edwards. *Netscape Time: The Making of the Billion-Dollar Start-up That Took on Microsoft.* New York: St. Martin's, 1999.

Clemente, Peter C. *State of the Net: The New Frontier.* New York: McGraw-Hill, 1998.

Cochran Entertainment. "PBS Life on the Internet: Timeline," *PBS.* http://www.pbs.org/internet/timeline/timeline-txt.html, 1997 [accessed 24 March 2000].

Coffey, Steve, and Horst Stipp. "The Interactions between Computer and Television Usage." *Journal of Advertising Research* 37, no. 2 (1997): 61-67.

Corbin, R. A. "The Development of the National Research and Education Network." *Information Technology and Libraries* 10, no. 3 (1991): 212-20.

Corman, Steven R. "Use and Uses of a Congressman's Network Information Services." *Internet Research: Electronic Networking Applications and Policy* 4, no. 4 (1994): 36-51.

Crang, Mike, Phil Crang, and Jon May. *Virtual Geographies: Bodies, Space, and Relations.* Sussex Studies in Culture and Communication. London: Routledge, 1999.

Creech, Bill. *The Five Pillars of TQM: How to Make Total Quality Management Work for You.* New York: Truman Talley Books/Dutton, 1994.

Cringely, Robert X., John Gau Productions, Oregon Public Broadcasting, Reiner Moritz Associates, Channel Four, and Public Broadcasting Service. *Triumph of the Nerds.* New York: Ambrose Video, 1996. Videorecording.

Croft, W. Bruce, and R. H. Thompson. "I³R: A New Approach to the Design of Document Retrieval Systems." *Journal of the American Society for Information Science* 38, no. 6 (1987): 389-404.

Crowston, Kevin, and Ericka Kammerer. "Communicative Style and Gender Differences in Computer-Mediated Communications." In *Cyberghetto or Cybertopia? Race, Class, and Gender on the Internet,* 185-203. Westport, Conn.: Praeger, 1998.

Curtis, Karen L., Ann C. Weller, and Julie M. Hurd. "Information-Seeking Behavior of Health Sciences Faculty: The Impact of New Information Technologies." *Bulletin of the Medical Library Association* 85, no. 4 (1997): 402-10.

Dalrymple, P. W. "Retrieval by Reformulation in Two Library Catalogs: Towards a Cognitive Model of Searching Behavior." *Journal of the American Society for Information Science* 41, no. 4 (1990): 272-81.

Davis, Fred D. "Perceived Usefulness, Perceived Ease of Use, and User Acceptance of Information Technology." *MIS Quarterly* 13, no. 3 (1989): 319-40.

———. "User Acceptance of Information Technology: System Characteristics, User Perceptions, and Behavioral Impacts." *International Journal of Man-Machine Studies* 38 (1993): 475-87.

Davis, Richard. *The Web of Politics: The Internet's Impact on the American Political System.* New York: Oxford University Press, 1999.

Dawson, Jeff. *Gay and Lesbian Online.* Los Angeles: Alyson Books, 1998.

de la Pena McCook, Kathleen, and Tosca O. Gonsalves. "The Research University and Education for Librarianship: Considerations for User-Centered Professionals in Libraries." In *Libraries as User-Centered Organizations: Imperatives for Organizational Change,* edited by Meredith A. Butler, 193-207. New York: Haworth Press, 1993.

De Mey, M. *The Cognitive Paradigm.* Dordrecht: Reidel, 1982.

De Mey, M. "The Cognitive Viewpoint: Its Development and Its Scope." In *International Workshop on the Cognitive Viewpoint,* edited by M. De Mey, xvi-xxxii. Ghent: University of Ghent, 1977.

Dempsey, Bert J., Robert C. Vreeland, Robert G. Sumner, and Kiduk Yang. "Design and Empirical Evaluation of Search Software for Legal Professionals on the WWW." *Information Processing and Management* 36, no. 2 (2000): 253-73.

Dempsey, L. "Research Networks and Academic Information Services: Towards an Academic Infrastructure: Part 1." *Journal of Information Networking* 1, no. 1 (1993): 1-17.

Dern, Daniel P. *The Internet Guide for New Users.* New York: McGraw-Hill, 1994.

Dervin, Brenda. "Information (If and Only If) Democracy: An Examination of Underlying Assumptions." *Journal of the American Society for Information Science* 45, no. 6 (1994): 369-85.

———. "Information Needs and Information Seeking: The Search for Questions behind the Research Agenda." Paper presented at the UCLA-NSF Workshop on Social Aspects of Digital Libraries, Los Angeles, 1996.

———. "On Studying Information Seeking Methodologically: The Implications of Connecting Metatheory to Method." *Information Processing and Management* 35, no. 6 (1999): 727-50.

Dervin, Brenda, and M. Nilan. "Information Needs and Uses." *Annual Review of Science and Technology* 21 (1986): 3-27.

D'Esposito, Joanne E., and Rachel M. Gardner. "University Students' Perceptions of the Internet: An Exploratory Study." *Journal of Academic Librarianship* 25, no. 6 (1999): 456-61.

Devlin, Brenda, and Mary Burke. "Internet: The Ultimate Reference Tool?" *Internet Research: Electronic Networking Applications and Policy* 7, no. 2 (1997): 101-8.

Dillon, A. *Designing Usable Electronic Text: Ergonomic Aspects of Human Information Usage.* London: Taylor and Francis, 1994.

Donthu, Naveen, and Adriana Garcia. "The Internet Shopper." *Journal of Advertising Research* 39, no. 3 (1999): 52-58.

Dosi, Giovanni. "Sources, Procedures, and Microeconomic Effects of Innovation." *Journal of Economic Literature* 26, no. 3 (1988): 1120-71.

Dresang, Eliza T. "More Research Needed: Informal Information-Seeking Behavior of Youth on the Internet." *Journal of the American Society for Information Science* 50, no. 12 (1999): 1123-24.

Ebo, Bosah L., ed. *Cyberghetto or Cybertopia? Race, Class, and Gender on the Internet.* Westport, Conn.: Praeger, 1998.

Eisenberg, M., and L. Schamber. "Relevance: The Search for a Definition." Paper presented at the 51st Annual Meeting of the American Society for Information Science, 1988.

Ellis, D. "A Behavioural Approach to Information System Design." *Journal of Documentation* 45, no. 3 (1989): 171-209.

———. "The Physical and Cognitive Paradigms in Information Retrieval Research." *Journal of Documentation* 48, no. 1 (1992): 45-64.

Ellis, R. Darin. "Patterns of E-Mail Requests by Users of an Internet-Based Aging-Services Information System." *Family Relations* 48, no. 1 (1999): 15-21.

Emmanouilides, Christos, and Kathy Hammond. "Internet Usage: Predictors of Active Users and Frequency of Use." *Journal of Interactive Marketing* 14, no. 2 (2000): 17-32.

Erdelez, Sandra, and Philip Doty. "Computing and Telecommunication Needs in Texas Rural Courts." *Computing and Telecommunication Needs in Texas Rural Courts.* http://www.courts.state.tx/jcit/rcourt.htm, September 1998 [accessed 29 November 2000].

Estrada, Susan. *Connecting to the Internet: A Buyer's Guide.* Sebastopol, Calif.: O'Reilly & Associates, 1993.

European Workshop IDMS '96. *Interactive Distributed Multimedia Systems and Services: European Workshop IDMS '96, Berlin, Germany, March 4-6, 1996.* Berlin: Springer, 1996.

Everard, Jerry. *Virtual States: The Internet and the Boundaries of the Nation-State, Technology, and Global Political Economy.* London: Routledge, 2000.

Ferguson, Charles H. *High Stakes, No Prisoners: A Winner's Tale of Greed and Glory in the Internet Wars.* New York: Times Business, 1999.

Fidel, Raya, Rachel K. Davies, Mary H. Douglass, Jenny K. Holder, Carla J. Hopkins, Elisabeth J. Kushner, Bryan K Miyagishima, and Christina D. Toney. "A Visit to the Information Mall: Web Searching Behavior of High School Students." *Journal of the American Society for Information Science* 50, no. 1 (1999): 24-37.

Fidel, Raya, and Efthimis Efthimiadis. "Content Organization and Retrieval Project, Phase I: A Work-Centered Examination of Web Searching Behavior of Boeing Engineers." Seattle: Boeing Company, 1998.

Finlay, Karen, and Thomas Finlay. "The Relative Roles of Knowledge and Innovativeness in Determining Librarians' Attitudes toward and Use of the Internet: A Structural Equation Modeling Approach." *Library Quarterly* 66, no. 1 (1996): 59-83.

Fisher, Sharon. *Riding the Internet Highway.* Carmel, Ind.: New Riders, 1993.

Ford, Nigel, and Dave Miller. "Gender Differences in Internet Perception and Use." *ASLIB Proceedings* 48, no. 7/8 (July/August 1996): 183-92.

Fram, Eugene H., and Dale B. Grady. "Internet Shoppers: Is There a Surfer Gender Gap?" *Direct Marketing* 59, no. 9 (1997): 46-50.

Furnell, S. M., and T. Karweni. "Security Implications of Electronic Commerce: A Survey of Consumers and Businesses." *Internet Research: Electronic Networking Applications and Policy* 9, no. 5 (1999): 372-82.

Furse, David H., Girish N. Punj, and David W. Stewart. "A Typology of Individual Search Strategies among Purchases of New Automobiles." *Journal of Consumer Research* 10 (1984): 417-31.

Gackenbach, Jayne. *Psychology and the Internet: Intrapersonal, Interpersonal, and Transpersonal Implications.* San Diego: Academic Press, 1998.

Gaines, Brian R., Lee Li-Jen Chen, and Mildred L. G. Shaw. "Modeling the Human Factors of Scholarly Communities Supported through the Internet and World Wide Web." *Journal of the American Society for Information Science* 48, no. 11 (1997): 987-1003.

Gallo, Michael A., and Phillip B. Horton. "Direct and Unrestricted Access to the Internet: A Case Study of an East Central Florida High School." *Educational Technology Research and Development* 42, no. 4 (1994): 17-39.

Gatignon, Hubert, and Thomas S. Robertson. "A Propositional Inventory for New Diffusion Research." *Journal of Consumer Research* 11 (1985): 849-67.

Geroski, P. A. "Models of Technology Diffusion." *Research Policy* 29 (2000): 603-25.

Gibson, Susan, and Dianne Oberg. "Learning to Use the Internet: A Study of Teacher Learning through Collaborative Research Partnerships." *Alberta Journal of Educational Research* 44, no. 2 (1998): 239-41.

Giguere, M. "An Introduction to Services Accessible on the Internet." *Education Libraries* 16, no. 2 (1992): 5-9.

Glasgow, Neal A. *New Curriculum for New Times: A Guide to Student-Centered, Problem-Based Learning.* Thousand Oaks, Calif.: Corwin Press, 1997.

Gomez, Carmen Mont. "The Social Uses of Internet in Mexico: A Case Study." *Telematics and Informatics* 16, no. 3 (1999): 91-98.

Gomez, Enrique J., Jose A. Quiles, Marcos F. Sanz, and Francisco del Pozo. "A User-Centered Cooperative Information System for Medical Imaging Diagnosis." *Journal of the American Society for Information Science* 49, no. 9 (1998): 810-16.

Gould, Cheryl. *Searching Smart on the World Wide Web: Tools and Techniques for Getting Quality Results.* Internet Workshop Series, No. 8. Berkeley, Calif.: Library Solutions Press, 1998.

Graphics, Visualization and Usability Center. "GVU's Tenth WWW User Survey." *GVU's WWW User Surveys.* http://www.gvu.gatech.edu/user_surveys/, October 1998 [accessed May 22, 2001].

Greeve, N., and D. E. Stanton. *AARNet Survey, 1991.* Perth, Australia: Greeve and Stanton, 1991.

Gregory, Vicki L., Marilyn H. Karrenbrock Stauffer, and Thomas W. Keene. *Multicultural Resources on the Internet.* Englewood, Colo.: Libraries Unlimited, 1999.

Griffiths, R. T. "Internet for Historians, History of the Internet, the Development of the Internet." http://www.let.leidenuniv.nl/history/ivh/INTERNET.HTM, 9 March 1999 [accessed 24 March 2000].

Gromov, Gregory R. "History of the Internet and WWW: The Roads and Crossroads of Internet History," *Internet Valley.*

http://www.internetvalley.com/intval.html, 2000 [accessed 24 March 2000].

Hack, Lisa, and Sue Smey. "A Survey of Internet Use by Teachers in Three Urban Connecticut Schools." *School Library Media Quarterly* 25, no. 3 (1997): 151-55.

Halpern, D., and M. Nilan. "A Step toward Shifting the Research Emphasis in Information Science from the System to the User: An Empirical Investigation of Source-Evaluation Behaviour Information Seeking and Use." Paper presented at the 51st Annual Meeting of the American Society for Information Science, 1988.

Harcourt, Wendy. *Women@Internet: Creating New Cultures in Cyberspace.* London: Zed Books, 1999.

Hardy, I. Trotter, and Library of Congress Copyright Office. *Project Looking Forward: Sketching the Future of Copyright in a Networked World: Final Report.* Washington, D.C.: Library of Congress Copyright Office, May 1998.

Harper, Christopher. *And That's the Way It Will Be: News and Information in a Digital World.* New York: New York University Press, 1998.

Harris, Cheryl. *An Internet Education: A Guide to Doing Research on the Internet.* Belmont, Calif.: Integrated Media Group, 1996.

Harris, Judith B., and Neal Grandgenett. "Correlates with Use of Telecomputing Tools: K-12 Teachers' Beliefs and Demographics." *Journal of Research on Computing in Education* 31, no. 4 (1999): 327-41.

Harris, Kimberly D., and James D. Campbell. "Internet by Proxy: How Rural Physicians Use the Internet." *Social Science Computer Review* 18, no. 4 (2000): 502-7.

He, Peter Wei, and Trudi E. Jacobson. "What Are They Doing with the Internet? A Study of User Information Seeking Behaviors." *Internet Reference Quarterly* 1, no. 1 (1996): 31-51.

Henry, Marcia Klinger, Linda Keenan, and Michael Reagan. *Search Sheets for OPACs on the Internet: A Selective Guide to U.S. OPACs Utilizing VT100 Emulation.* Westport, Conn.: Meckler, 1991.

Hewins, E. T. "Information Need and Use Studies." *Annual Review of Science and Technology* 25 (1990): 145-72.

Hill, Janette R. "The World Wide Web as a Tool for Information Retrieval: An Exploratory Study of Users' Strategies in an Open-Ended System." *School Library Media Quarterly* 25 (Summer 1997): 229-36.

Hill, Kevin A., and John E. Hughes. *Cyberpolitics: Citizen Activism in the Age of the Internet (People, Passions, and Power)*. Lanham, Md.: Rowman & Littlefield, 1998.

Hiott, Judith. "Making Online Use Count." *Library Journal*, October 1, 1999: 44-47.

Hirsch, E. D., Jr. "'You Can Always Look It Up' . . . Or Can You?" *American Educator* 24, no. 1 (2000): 4-9.

Holeton, Richard. *Composing Cyberspace: Identity, Community, and Knowledge in the Electronic Age*. Boston: McGraw-Hill, 1998.

Hollands, William D. *Teaching the Internet to Library Staff and Users: Ten Ready-to-Go Workshops That Work*. New York: Neal-Schuman, 1999.

Howe, Walt. "A Brief History of the Internet," *Walt Howe's Internet Learning Center*. http://www.walthowe.com/navnet/history.html, 13 April 2001 [accessed 27 July 2001].

Hwang, Ching-Shyang. "A Comparative Study of Tax-Filing Methods: Manual, Internet, and Two-Dimensional Bar Code." *Journal of Government Information* 27, no. 2 (2000): 113-27.

Ingwersen, Peter. "A Cognitive View of Three Selected Online Search Facilities." *Online Review* 8, no. 5 (1984): 465-92.

———. *Information Retrieval Interaction*. London: Taylor Graham, 1992.

———. "Search Procedures in the Library: Analysed from the Cognitive Point of View." *Journal of Documentation* 38, no. 3 (1982): 165-91.

Janes, J. W. "Relevance Judgments and the Incremental Presentation of Document Presentations." *Information Processing and Management* 27, no. 6 (1991): 629-46.

Johnson, Steven. *Interface Culture: How New Technology Transforms the Way We Create and Communicate*. San Francisco: Harper-Edge, 1997.

Jones, Joseph M., and Leo R. Vijayasarathy. "Internet Consumer Catalog Shopping: Findings from an Exploratory Study and Directions for Future Research." *Internet Research: Electronic Networking Applications and Policy* 8, no. 4 (1998): 322-30.

Jones, Steve. *Virtual Culture: Identity and Communication in Cybersociety*. London: Sage Publications, 1997.

Kafai, Yasmin B., and Sharon Sutton. "Elementary School Students' Computer and Internet Use at Home: Current Trends and Issues." *Journal of Educational Computing Research* 21, no. 3 (1999): 345-62.

Kahin, B. "Information Technology and Information Infrastructure." In *Empowering Technology: Implementing a U.S. Strategy*, edited by L. M. Branscomb, 135-66. Cambridge, Mass.: MIT Press, 1993.

———. "The Internet and the National Information Infrastructure." In *Public Access to the Internet*, edited by B. Kahin and J. Keller, 3-23. Cambridge, Mass.: MIT Press, 1995.

Kaminer, Noam. "Scholars and the Use of the Internet." *Library and Information Science Research* 19, no. 4 (1997): 329-45.

Kandell, Jonathan J. "Internet Addiction on Campus: The Vulnerability of College Students." *CyberPsychology and Behavior* 1, no. 1 (1998): 11-17.

Katz, James, and Phillip Aspden. "Motivations for and Barriers to Internet Usage: Results of a National Public Opinion Survey." *Internet Research: Electronic Networking Applications and Policy* 7, no. 3 (1997): 170-88.

Keating, Anne B., and Joseph Hargitai. *The Wired Professor: A Guide to Incorporating the World Wide Web in College Instruction*. New York: New York University Press, 1999.

Kehoe, Brendan P. *Zen and the Art of the Internet: A Beginner's Guide*. 3d ed. Englewood Cliffs, N.J.: PTR Prentice Hall, 1994.

Kelly, Sarah, and David Nicholas. "Is the Business Cybrarian a Reality? Internet Use in Business Libraries." *ASLIB Proceedings* 48, no. 5 (1996): 136-44.

Kennedy, Lynn, Charles Cole, and Susan Carter. "Connecting Online Search Strategies and Information Needs: A User-Centered, Focus-Labeling Approach." *Reference Quarterly* 36, no. 4 (1997): 562-68.

Keyes, Jessica. *Internet Management*. Boca Raton, Fla.: Auerbach, 2000.

Kibirige, Harry M., and Lisa DePalo. "The Internet as a Source of Academic Research Information: Findings of Two Pilot Studies." *Information Technology and Libraries* 19, no. 1 (2000): 11-16.

Kingsley, Paul, and Terry Anderson. "Facing Life without the Internet." *Internet Research: Electronic Networking Applications and Policy* 8, no. 4 (1998): 303-12.

Kirriemuir, John. "OMNI: Accessing the Internet." *Ariadne (Online)* 20 (1999).

Kizza, Joseph Migga. *Civilizing the Internet: Global Concerns and Efforts toward Regulation*. Jefferson, N.C.: McFarland, 1998.

Klobas, Jane E. "Networked Information Resources: Electronic Opportunities for Users and Librarians." *OCLC Systems and Services* 13, no. 1 (1997): 25-34.

Knowles, Malcolm Shepherd. *The Modern Practice of Adult Education: From Pedagogy to Andragogy.* Chicago: Association Press, 1980.

Kochmer, Jonathan, and Northwest Academic Computing Consortium. *Internet Passport: NorthWestNet's Guide to Our World Online.* 4th ed. Bellevue, Wash.: Northwest Academic Computing Consortium, 1993.

Kolko, Beth E., Lisa Nakamura, and Gilbert B. Rodman. *Race in Cyberspace.* New York: Routledge, 2000.

Kollmann, Tobias. "Measuring the Acceptance of Electronic Marketplaces: A Study Based on a Used-Car Trading Site." *Journal of Computer-Mediated Communication* 6, no. 2 (2001).

Korgaonkar, Pradeep K., and Lori D. Wolin. "A Multivariate Analysis of Web Usage." *Journal of Advertising Research* 39, no. 2 (1999): 53-68.

Kosmin, L. J. "Library Reference Resources: The Internet Challenge." Paper presented at Online Information '91, London, December 10-12, 1991.

Kovacs, Diane K., Kara L. Robinson, and Jeanne Dixon. "Scholarly E-Conferences on the Academic Networks: How Library and Information Science Professionals Use Them." *Journal of the American Society for Information Science* 46, no. 4 (1995): 244-53.

Kraut, R., William Scherlis, Tridas Mukhopadhyay, Jane Manning, and Sara Kiesler. "The Home Net Field Trial of Residential Internet Services." *Communications of the ACM* 39, no. 12 (1996): 55-63.

Krol, Ed. *The Whole Internet: User's Guide and Catalog.* Sebastopol, Calif.: O'Reilly & Associates, 1993.

Krol, Ed, and Paula M. Ferguson. *The Whole Internet for Windows 95: User's Guide and Catalog.* Sebastopol, Calif.: O'Reilly & Associates, 1995.

Krol, Ed, and Michael Kosta Loukides. *The Whole Internet User's Guide and Catalog.* 2d ed. Sebastopol, Calif.: O'Reilly & Associates, 1994.

Kuhlthau, Carol Collier. "Inside the Search Process: Information Seeking from the User's Perspective." *Journal of the American Society for Information Science* 42, no. 5 (1991): 361-71.

Kuhlthau, Carol Collier, Betty J. Turock, and Robert J. Belvin. "Facilitating Information Seeking through Cognitive Models of the Search Process." Paper presented at the 51st Annual Meeting of the American Society for Information Science, 1988.

Kurz, Raymond A. *Internet and the Law: Legal Fundamentals for the Internet User.* Rockville, Md.: Government Institutes, 1996.

LaFerle, Carrie, Steven M. Edwards, and Wei-Na Lee. "Teens' Use of Traditional Media and the Internet." *Journal of Advertising Research* 40, no. 3 (2000): 55-65.

LaQuey, Tracy L. *The Internet Companion Plus: A Beginner's Start-up Kit for Global Networking.* 2d ed. Reading, Mass.: Addison-Wesley, 1994.

Laskowski, Mary Schneider. "The Impact of Electronic Access to Government Information: What Users and Documents Specialists Think." *Journal of Government Information* 27, no. 2 (2000): 173-85.

Latour, Bruno. *Pandora's Hope: Essays on the Reality of Science Studies.* Cambridge, Mass.: Harvard University Press, 1999.

Lazinger, Susan S., Judit Bar-Ilan, and Bluma C. Peritz. "Internet Use by Faculty Members in Various Disciplines: A Comparative Case Study." *Journal of the American Society for Information Science* 48, no. 6 (1997): 508-18.

Learn, L. L. "Networks: A Review of Their Technology, Architecture, and Implementation." *Library Hi Tech* 6, no. 2 (1988): 43.

Lederer, Albert L., Donna J. Maupin, Mark P. Sena, and Youlong Zhuang. "The Technology Acceptance Model and the World Wide Web." *Decision Support Systems* 29 (2000): 269-82.

Leiner, Barry M., Vinton G. Cerf, David D. Clark, Robert E. Kahn, Leonard Kleinrock, Daniel C. Lynch, Jon Postel, Larry G. Roberts, and Stephen Wolff. "A Brief History of the Internet (3.1)." *Internet Society (ISOC).* http://www.isoc.org/internet-history/brief.html, 20 February 1998 [accessed 17 March 2000].

Leonard-Barton, Dorothy, and Isabelle DesChamps. "Managerial Influence in the Implementation of New Technology." *Management Science* 34, no. 10 (1988): 1252-65.

Liebscher, Peter, Eileen G. Abels, and Daniel W. Denman. "Factors That Influence the Use of Electronic Networks by Science and Engineering Faculty at Small Institutions, Part II: Preliminary Use Indicators." *Journal of the American Society for Information Science* 48, no. 6 (1997): 496-507.

Litan, Robert E., and William A. Niskanen. *Going Digital! A Guide to Policy in the Digital Age.* Washington, D.C.: Brookings Institution Press and Cato Institute, 1998.

Logan, Rochelle. "Colorado Librarian Internet Use: Results of a Survey." *School Library Media Quarterly.* http://www.ala.org/aasl/SLMQ/logan.html, 8 June 1998 [accessed 21 October 2000].

Loh, Lawrence, and Yee-Shyuan Ong. "The Adoption of Internet-Based Stock Trading: A Conceptual Framework and Empirical Results." *Journal of Information Technology* 13, no. 2 (1998): 81-94.

Lubans, John, Jr. "How First-Year University Students Use and Regard Internet Resources." *Duke University*. http://www.lib.duke.edu/lubans/docs/1styear/firstyear.html, 8 April 1998 [accessed 12 December 2000].

———. "Key Findings on Internet Use among Students." *Duke University*. http://www.lib.duke.edu/lubans/docs/key/key.html, 5 March 1999 [accessed 13 May 2001].

———. "When Students Hit the Surf: What Kids Really Do on the Internet and What They Want from Librarians." *School Library Journal* (September 1999): 144-47.

Lynch, Clifford A., and Cecilia M. Preston. "Evolution of Networked Information Resources." Paper presented at the 12th National Online Meeting, New York, May 7-9, 1991.

———. "Internet Access to Information Resources." In *Annual Review of Information Science and Technology*, edited by Martha E. Williams, 263-312. Amsterdam: Elsevier Science Publishers, 1990.

Maehl, William H. *Lifelong Learning at Its Best: Innovative Practices in Adult Credit Programs*. San Francisco: Jossey-Bass, 2000.

Mahajan, Vijay, Eitan Muller, and Frank M. Bass. "New Product Diffusion Models in Marketing: A Review and Directions for Research." *Journal of Marketing* 54 (1990): 1-26.

Mahling, D. E. "Cognitive Systems Engineering for Visualization." In *Cognitive Aspects of Visual Languages and Visual Interfaces*, edited by M. J. Tauber, D. E. Mahling, and F. Arefi, 41-75. Amsterdam: North-Holland, 1994.

Marchionini, Gary. "Interfaces for End-User Information Seeking." *Journal of the American Society for Information Science* 43, no. 2 (1992): 156-63.

Margaria, Tiziana. *Services and Visualization: Towards User-Friendly Design*. Berlin: Springer, 1998.

Marlow, Eugene. *Web Visions: An Inside Look at Successful Business Strategies on the Net*. New York: Van Nostrand Reinhold, 1997.

Martin, Lyn Elizabeth M. *The Challenge of Internet Literacy: The Instruction-Web Convergence*. New York: Haworth Press, 1997.

Martin, Shelley. "Internet Use in the Classroom: The Impact of Gender." *Social Science Computer Review* 16, no. 4 (1998): 411-18.

Mates, Barbara T., Doug Wakefield, and Judith M. Dixon. *Adaptive Technology for the Internet: Making Electronic Resources Accessible to All*. Chicago: American Library Association, 2000.

McArthur, David, Matthew W. Lewis, and Rand Education Institute. *Untangling the Web: Applications of the Internet and Other Information Technologies to Higher Learning.* Santa Monica: Rand, 1998.

McClure, Charles R. *Statement to the U.S. Congress, House of Representatives Committee on Science Space and Technology Subcommittee on Science.* Syracuse, N.Y.: Syracuse University, 1994.

McClure, Charles R., Ann P. Bishop, Philip Doty, and Howard Rosenbaum. *The National Research and Education Network (NREN): Research and Policy Perspectives.* Norwood, N.J.: Ablex Publishing, 1991.

McClure, Charles R., William E. Moen, and J. Ryan. "Academic Libraries and the Impact of Internet/NREN: Key Issues and Findings." Paper presented at the 56th Annual Meeting of the American Society for Information Science, 1993.

McFarland, Lynne J., Larry E. Senn, and John Childress. *Twenty-First Century Leadership.* Los Angeles: Leadership Press, 1994.

McGraw, Gary, and Edward Felten. *Java Security.* New York: Wiley, 1997.

McLaughlin, Ruth. "The Internet and Japanese Education: The Effect of Globalisation on Education Policies and Government Initiatives." *ASLIB Proceedings* 51, no. 7 (1999): 224-32.

McLoughlin, Glenn J. "Next Generation Internet and Related Initiatives." *Journal of Academic Librarianship* 25, no. 3 (1999): 226-31.

McMurdo, George. "Electric Writing: The Net by Numbers." *Journal of Information Science* 22, no. 5 (1996): 381-90.

McQuivey, James L. "How the Web Was Won: The Commercialization of Cyberspace." In *Cyberghetto or Cybertopia? Race, Class, and Gender on the Internet,* edited by Bosah Ebo, 83-99. Westport, Conn.: Praeger, 1998.

Mitchell, Felicia. "Internet Use and Gender and Emory and Henry College: A Survey of Student Users." *College and Undergraduate Libraries* 5, no. 2 (1998): 1-9.

Moen, William E., Charles R. McClure, J. Koelker, and E. Stewart. "Assessing the Government Information Locator Service (GILS): A Multi-Method Approach for Evaluating Networked Services." Paper presented at the 60th Annual Meeting of the American Society for Information Science, 1997.

Moore, Gary C., and Izak Benbasat. "Development of an Instrument to Measure the Perceptions of Adopting an Information Technology

Innovation." *Information Systems Research* 2, no. 3 (1991): 192-222.

Morahan-Martin, J., and P. Schumacher. "Incidence and Correlates of Pathological Internet Use among College Students." *Computers in Human Behavior* 16, no. 1 (2000): 13-29.

Morgan, Eric Lease. *WAIS and Gopher Servers: A Guide for Internet End-Users*. Westport, Conn.: Mecklermedia, 1994.

Morris, Ruth C. T. "Toward a User-Centered Information Service." *Journal of the American Society for Information Science* 45, no. 1 (1994): 20-30.

M. S. Knowles & Associates. *Andragogy in Action: Applying Modern Principles of Adult Learning*. San Francisco: Jossey-Bass, 1985.

Nachmias, Rafi, David Mioduser, and Anat Shemla. "Internet Usage by Students in an Israeli High School." *Journal of Educational Computing Research* 22, no. 1 (2000): 55-73.

Nahl, Diane. "Learning the Internet and the Structure of Information Behavior." *Journal of the American Society for Information Science* 49, no. 11 (1998): 1017-23.

———. "The User-Centered Revolution: 1970-1995." In *Encyclopedia of Library and Information Science*, edited by Allen Kent, 313-71. New York: Marcel Dekker, 1998.

Nardi, Bonnie A., and Vicki O'Day. *Information Ecologies: Using Technology with Heart*. Cambridge, Mass.: MIT Press, 1999.

Nasser, Thomas-Olivier, and World Bank Private Participation in Infrastructure Group. *Congestion Pricing and Network Expansion*. Washington, D.C.: World Bank Private Sector Development Department Private Participation in Infrastructure Group, 1998.

National Center for Education Statistics. *Internet Access in Public Schools*. Washington, D.C.: U.S. Dept. of Education, Office of Educational Research and Improvement, 1998.

Newby, Gregory B. "User Models in Information Retrieval: Applying Knowledge about Human Communication to Computer Interface Design." Paper presented at the 52nd Annual Meeting of the American Society for Information Science, 1989.

Nicholas, D., and D. Fenton. "The Internet and the Changing Information Environment." *Managing Information* 4, no. 1/2 (1997): 30-33.

Nicholas, David, Paul Huntington, Peter Williams, Nat Lievesley, Tom Dobrowolski, and Richard Withey. "Developing and Testing Methods to Determine Use of Web Sites: Case Study Newspapers." *ASLIB Proceedings* 51, no. 5 (1999): 144-54.

Nims, Julia K., and Linda Rich. "How Successfully Do Users Search the Web?" *College and Research Libraries News* 59, no. 3 (1998): 155-58.

"No Gain without Pain: Why the Transition to E-Government Will Hurt." *Economist*, June 22, 2000.

Norman, Donald A. "Cognitive Engineering." In *User-Centered System Design: New Perspectives on Human-Computer Interaction*, edited by Donald A. Norman and Stephen W. Draper, 31-61. Hillsdale, N.J.: Lawrence Erlbaum Associates, 1986.

————. "Toward Human-Centered Design." *Technology Review* 96 (1993): 47-53.

————. *Turn Signals Are the Facial Expressions of Automobiles*. Reading, Mass.: Addison-Wesley, 1992.

Norman, Donald A., and Stephen W. Draper, eds. *User-Centered System Design: New Perspectives on Human-Computer Interaction*. Hillsdale, N.J.: Lawrence Erlbaum Associates, 1986.

O'Keefe, Robert M., Melissa Cole, Patrick Y. K. Chau, Ann Massey, Mitzi Montoya-Weiss, and Mark Perry. "From the User Interface to the Consumer Interface: Results from a Global Experiment." *International Journal of Human-Computer Studies* 52, no. 4 (2000): 611-28.

Olson, G. M., and J. S. Olson. "User-Centered Design of Collaboration Technology." *Journal of Organizational Computing* 1, no. 1 (1991): 61-83.

Olson, Truda. "University Reference Librarians Using Internet: A Survey." *Australian Academic and Research Libraries* 26, no. 3 (1995): 188-91.

Onvural, Raif O., Seyhan Civanlar, and James V. Luciani, eds. *Internet II: Quality of Service and Future Directions: Proceedings of SPIE (International Society for Optical Engineers), 20-21 September 1999, Boston, Massachusetts*. Bellingham, Wash.: SPIE, 1999.

O'Reilly & Associates. *The Harvard Conference on the Internet and Society*. Sebastopol, Calif.: O'Reilly & Associates, 1997.

Patrick, Andrew S., and Alex Black. "Who Is Going Online? Results from the National Capital FreeNet." *Internet Research: Electronic Networking Applications and Policy* 7, no. 4 (1997): 305-19.

Pattinson, Hugh, and Linden Brown. "Chameleons in Marketplace: Industry Transformation in the New Electronic Marketing Environment." *Internet Research: Electronic Networking Applications and Policy* 6, no. 2/3 (1996): 31-40.

Peck, Robert S. *Libraries, the First Amendment, and Cyberspace: What You Need to Know*. Chicago: American Library Association, 2000.

Peha, Jon M. "How K-12 Teachers Are Using Computer Networks." *Educational Leadership* 53, no. 2 (1995): 18-25.

Pelzer, Nancy L., William H. Wiese, and Joan M. Leysen. "Library Use and Information-Seeking Behavior of Veterinary Medical Students Revisited in the Electronic Environment." *Bulletin of the Medical Library Association* 86, no. 3 (1998): 346-53.

Perry, Clifford. "Travelers on the Internet: A Survey of Internet Users." *Online* 19 (March/April 1995): 29-30.

Perry, Timothy T., Leslie Anne Perry, and Karen Hosack-Curlin. "Internet Use by University Students: An Interdisciplinary Study on Three Campuses." *Internet Research: Electronic Networking Applications and Policy* 8, no. 2 (1998): 136-41.

Persson, Eric, Linda Tsantis, and Barbara L. Kurshan. *Netpower: Resource Guide to Online Computer Services: Using Online Information for Business, Education, and Research.* Lancaster, Pa.: Fox Chapel, 1993.

Pettigrew, Karen. "Lay Information Provision in Community Settings: How Community Health Nurses Disseminate Human Services Information to the Elderly." *Library Quarterly* 70, no. 1 (2000): 47-85.

Pettigrew, Karen, Raya Fidel, and Harry Bruce. "Conceptual Frameworks in Information Behavior." *Annual Review of Information Science and Technology* 35 (2001).

Pettit, Sue. "Internet Use by U.K. Academic Law Librarians." *Law Librarian* 26, no. 1 (1995): 269-71.

Phau, Ian, and Sui Meng Poon. "Factors Influencing the Types of Products and Services Purchased over the Internet." *Internet Research: Electronic Networking Applications and Policy* 10, no. 2 (2000): 102-13.

Pinter, Ron Yair, and Shalom Tsur. *Next-Generation Information Technology and Systems: Proceedings of the Fourth International Workshop, Zikhron-Ya'akov, Israel, July 1999.* Berlin: Springer, 1999.

Pitkow, James E., and Colleen M. Kehoe. "Results from the Graphics, Visualization, and Usability Center's Fourth WWW User Survey." *GVU User Surveys.* http://www.cc.gatech.edu/gvu/user_surveys/survey-10-1995, 1995 [accessed 8 June 2001].

Plas, Jeanne M. *Person-Centered Leadership: An American Approach to Participatory Management.* Thousand Oaks, Calif.: Sage, 1996.

Pliskin, Nava, and Celia T. Romm. "Empowering Effects of Electronic Group Communication." Working paper no. 6. Wollongong, Australia: University of Wollongong, 1994.

Porter, David. *Internet Culture.* New York: Routledge, 1997.

Price, Monroe Edwin. *The V-Chip Debate: Content Filtering from Television to the Internet.* Lea's Communication Series. Mahwah, N.J.: Erlbaum, 1998.

Quarterman, John S. *The Matrix: Computer Networks and Conferencing Systems Worldwide.* Bedford, Mass.: Digital Press, 1990.

Quittner, Joshua, Michelle Slatalla, and Netscape Communications Corporation. *Speeding the Net: The Inside Story of Netscape and How It Challenged Microsoft.* New York: Atlantic Monthly Press, 1998.

Rainie, Lee, and Dan Packel. "More Online, Doing More." Washington, D.C.: The Pew Internet and American Life Project, 2001.

Ren, Wen-Hua. "U.S. Government Information Need, Awareness, and Searching: A Study of Small Business Executives." *Journal of Government Information* 26, no. 5 (1999): 453-65.

Ricci, Andrea. "Towards a Systematic Study of Internet-Based Political and Social Communication in Europe." *Telematics and Informatics* 15, no. 3 (1998): 135-61.

Richardson, John, and Alison Shaw, eds. *The Body in Qualitative Research.* Brookfield, Vt.: Ashgate, 1998.

Rogers, Everett M. *Diffusion of Innovations.* 3d ed. New York: Free Press, 1983.

Ronfeldt, David F., and Arroyo Center. *The Zapatista "Social Netwar" in Mexico.* Santa Monica, Calif.: Rand, 1998.

Rosenthal, Marilyn, and Marsha Spiegelman. "Evaluating Use of the Internet among Academic Reference Librarians." *Internet Reference Services Quarterly* 1, no. 1 (1996): 53-67.

Rowand, Cassandra. *Internet Access in Public Schools and Classrooms, 1994-98.* Washington, D.C.: National Center for Education Statistics, 1999.

———. "Teacher Use of Computers and the Internet in Public Schools: Stats in Brief." Washington, D.C.: National Center for Education Statistics, 2000.

Salomon, G. "AI in Reverse: Computer Tools That Turn Cognitive." *Journal of Educational Computing Research* 4, no. 2 (1988): 123-39.

Sandstrom, Pamela E. "An Optimal Foraging Approach to Information Seeking and Use." *Library Quarterly* 64, no. 4 (1994): 414-49.

Sandvig, Christian. "The Internet Disconnect in Children's Policy: A User Study of Outcomes for Internet Access Subsidies and Content Regulation." Paper presented at the 28th Conference on Communication, Information, and Internet Policy, Alexandria, Virginia, 2000.

Saracevic, Tefko, and Paul Kantor. "A Study of Information Seeking and Retrieving, II: Users, Questions, and Effectiveness." *Journal of the American Society for Information Science* 39, no. 3 (1988): 177-96.

―――. "A Study of Information Seeking and Retrieving, III: Searchers, Searches, and Overlap." *Journal of the American Society for Information Science* 39, no. 3 (1988): 197-216.

Saracevic, Tefko, Paul Kantor, Alice Y. Chamis, and Donna Trivison. "A Study of Information Seeking and Retrieving. I: Background and Methodology." *Journal of the American Society for Information Science* 39, no. 3 (1988): 161-76.

Savolainen, Reijo. "Embarking on the Internet: What Motivates People?" *ASLIB Proceedings* 52, no. 5 (2000): 185-93.

―――. "Everyday Life Information Seeking: Approaching Information Seeking in the Context of Way of Life." *Library and Information Science Research* 17, no. 3 (1995): 259-94.

―――. "The Internet through Finnish Eyes: Citizens' Views on Electronic Networks." *Scandinavian Public Library Quarterly* 32, no. 3 (1999): 32-34.

―――. "The Role of the Internet in Information Seeking; Putting the Networked Services in Context." *Information Processing and Management* 35, no. 6 (1999): 765-82.

―――. "The Sense-Making Theory: Reviewing the Interests of a User-Centered Approach to Information Seeking and Use." *Information Processing and Management* 29, no. 1 (1993): 13-28.

Scarlett, Joanna. "Internet Use Survey." *The Law Librarian* 28, no. 2 (1997): 101-6.

Schacter, John, Gregory K. W. K. Chung, and Aimee Dorr. "Children's Internet Searching on Complex Problems: Performance and Process Analyses." *Journal of the American Society for Information Science* 49, no. 9 (1998): 840-49.

Scherer, Kathy. "College Life On-Line: Healthy and Unhealthy Internet Use." *Journal of College Student Development* 38, no. 6 (1997): 655-65.

Schlosser, Ann E., Sharon Shavitt, and Alaina Kafner. "Survey of Users' Attitudes toward Internet Advertising." *Journal of Interactive Marketing* 13, no. 3 (1999): 34-54.

Segaller, Stephen. *Nerds 2.0.1: A Brief History of the Internet.* New York: TV Books, 1998.

Shaw, Wendy. "The Use of the Internet by English Academics." *Information Research*. http://www.shef.ac.uk/~is/publications/infres/isic/shaw.html, 3 February 1999 [accessed 15 May 2001].

Shirato, Linda. *The Impact of Technology on Library Instruction: Papers and Session Materials Presented at the Twenty-First National LOEX Library Instruction Conference Held in Racine, Wisconsin, 14 to 15 May 1993.* Ann Arbor, Mich.: Pierian Press, 1995.

Simon, Scott, Andrew Cochran, Robert Duncan, Rae Hull, Melissa Sykes, Discovery Channel, Georgia Public Television, Cochran Entertainment, and PBS Video. *Life on the Internet.* Alexandria, Va.: PBS Video, 1997. Videorecording.

Singh, Supriya, and Annette Ryan. "Gender, Design, and Internet Commerce." *Internet Research: Electronic Networking Applications and Policy* 10, no. 1 (2000): 83-87.

Smith, Gerry. "Business Librarians Embrace the Internet: Annual Business Information Resources Survey." *Business Information Review* 14, no. 1 (1997): 1-14.

Staninger, Steven W., Susan Riehm Goshorn, Jennifer C. Boettcher, and Reference and American Library Association User Services Association. *Key Business Sources of the U.S. Government.* Chicago: American Library Association Reference and User Services Association, 1998.

Stefik, Mark. *Internet Dreams: Archetypes, Myths, and Metaphors.* Cambridge, Mass.: MIT Press, 1996.

Stephenson, Christie. "Recent Developments in Cultural Heritage Image Databases: Directions for User-Centered Design." *Library Trends* 48, no. 2 (1999): 410-37.

Stock, Gregory N., and Mohan V. Tatikonda. "A Typology of Project-Level Technology Transfer Process." *Journal of Operations Management* 18 (2000): 719-37.

Stover, Mark. "Reference Librarians and the Internet: A Qualitative Study." *Reference Services Review* 28, no. 1 (2000): 39-46.

Sudweeks, Fay, Margaret L. McLaughlin, and Sheizaf Rafaeli. *Network and Netplay: Virtual Groups on the Internet.* Menlo Park, Calif.: AAAI Press, 1998.

Sugar, William. "User-Centered Perspective of Information Retrieval Research and Analysis Methods." In *Annual Review of Information Science and Technology*, edited by Martha E. Williams, 77-109. Medford, N.J.: Information Today, 1995.

Sultan, Fareena, and Lillian Chan. "The Adoption of New Technology: The Case of Object-Oriented Computing in Software Companies."

IEEE Transactions on Engineering Management 47, no. 1 (2000): 106-26.

Tafti, Mohammed H. A., and Ashraf I. Shirani. "Patterns of Use and Prospects for Adoption of the Internet Technology: An Empirical Study." *Journal of Computer Information Systems* 38, no. 1 (1997): 104-11.

Takacs, James, W. Michael Reed, John G. Wells, and Lynn A. Dombrowski. "The Effects of Online Multimedia Project Development, Learning Style, and Prior Computer Experiences on Teachers' Attitude toward the Internet and Hypermedia." *Journal of Research on Computing in Education* 31, no. 4 (1999): 341-55.

Talja, Sanna. "Constituting 'Information' and 'User' as Research Objects: A Theory of Knowledge Formations as an Alternative to the Information Man-Theory." Paper presented at the Information Seeking in Context Conference, Tampere, Finland, August 14-16, 1996.

Taylor, R. S. "Question-Negotiation and Information Seeking in Libraries." *College and Research Libraries* 29, no. 3 (1968): 178-94.

Taylor, Shirley, and Peter A. Todd. "Understanding Information Technology Usage: A Test of Competing Models." *Information Systems Research* 6, no. 2 (1995): 144-76.

Teo, Thompson S. H. "Differential Effects of Occupation on Internet Usage." *Internet Research: Electronic Networking Applications and Policy* 8, no. 2 (1998): 156-65.

Teo, Thompson S. H., and Vivien K. Lim. "Gender Differences in Internet Usage and Task Preference." *Behaviour and Information Technology* 19, no. 4 (2000): 283-95.

Tillotson, Joy, Joan Cherry, and Marshall Clinton. "Internet Use through the University of Toronto Library: Demographics, Destinations, and Users' Reactions." *Information Technology and Libraries* 14 (September 1995): 190-98.

Tomlins, Christopher L., and American Council of Leaned Societies. *Wave of the Present: The Scholarly Journal on the Edge of the Internet.* New York: American Council of Learned Societies, 1998.

Tornatzky, L. G., and K. J. Klein. "Innovation Characteristics and Innovation Adoption-Implementation: A Meta-Analysis of Findings." *IEEE Transactions on Engineering Management* EM-29, no. 1 (1982): 28-45.

Tuominen, Kimmo. "User-Centered Discourse: An Analysis of the Subject Positions of the User and the Librarian." *Library Quarterly* 67, no. 4 (1997): 350-71.

Turkle, Sherry. *Life on the Screen: Identity in the Age of the Internet.* New York: Simon & Schuster, 1995.

————. *The Second Self: Computers and the Human Spirit.* New York: Simon & Schuster, 1984.

Turner, Katherine, and Margaret Kendall. "Public Use of the Internet at Chester Library." *Information Research.* http://www.shef.ac.uk/ ~is/publications/infres/paper75.html, 2000 [accessed 15 May 2001].

United Nations. *United Nations Treaty Collection.* New York: United Nations, 1996. Computer program.

United States Congress. Senate. Committee on Commerce, Science, and Transportation. Subcommittee on Communications. *Internet 2 and "Next Generation Internet": Hearing before the Subcommittee on Communications of the Committee on Commerce, Science, and Transportation.* 105th Cong., 1st sess., 1997.

United States Congress. Senate. Special Committee on Aging. *Older Americans and the Worldwide Web: The New Wave of Internet Users.* Forum before the Special Committee on Aging. 105th Cong., 2d sess., 1998.

United States Department of Commerce. Information Infrastructure Taskforce. *National Information Infrastructure: Agenda for Action.* Washington, D.C.: United States Department of Commerce, Information Infrastructure Taskforce, 1993.

United States Department of Commerce. National Telecommunications and Information Administration. *Falling through the Net: Defining the Digital Divide: A Report on the Telecommunications and Information Technology Gap in America.* Washington, D.C.: United States Department of Commerce, National Telecommunications and Information Administration, 1999.

United States Department of the Interior. United States Geological Survey. *Connecting to the Internet.* Reston, Va.: United States Department of the Interior, United States Geological Survey, 1994. Videorecording.

United States Federal Networking Council. "Federal Networking Council Resolution: Definition of 'Internet.'" *National Coordination Office for Information Technology Research and Development.* http://www.itrd.gov/fnc/Internet_res.html, 30 October 1995 [accessed 2 July 2001].

United States Federal Trade Commission. Bureau of Consumer Protection. "Online Profiling: A Report to Congress." http://www.ftc. gov/os/2000/06/onlineprofilingreportjune2000.pdf, June 2000 [accessed 1 March 2001].

United States Internet Council and International Technology and Trade Associates, Inc. *State of the Internet, 2000.* Washington, D.C.: United States Internet Council, 2000.

United States National Commission on Libraries and Information Science. *Kids and the Internet: The Promise and the Perils: A National Commission of Libraries and Information Science Hearing in Arlington, Virginia, November 10, 1998.* http://www.nclis.gov/info/kids2.html, April 1999 [accessed 15 January 2001].

United States Library of Congress. Geography and Map Division. "Panoramic Maps, 1847-1921," *American Memory: Library of Congress.* http://lcweb2.loc.gov/ammem/pmhtml/panhome.html [accessed 31 August 2000].

United States National Research Council. NRENAISSANCE Committee. *Realizing the Information Future: The Internet and Beyond.* Washington, D.C.: National Academy Press, 1994.

Vanfossen, Phillip J. "Degree of Internet/WWW Use and Barriers to Use among Secondary Social Studies Teachers." *International Journal of Instructional Media* 28, no. 1 (2001): 57-74.

Veldof, Jerilyn R., Michael J. Prasse, and Victoria A. Mills. "Chauffeured by the User: Usability in the Electronic Library." *Journal of Library Administration* 26, no. 3/4 (1999): 115-40.

Vince, John, and Rae A. Earnshaw. *Virtual Worlds on the Internet.* Los Alamitos, Calif.: IEEE Computer Society, 1998.

Voorbij, Henk J. "Searching Scientific Information on the Internet: A Dutch Academic User Survey." *Journal of the American Society for Information Science* 50, no. 7 (1999): 598-615.

Wall, David S., and Jennifer Johnstone. "Lawyers, Information Technology, and Legal Practice: The Use of Information Technology by Provincial Lawyers." *International Review of Law, Computers, and Technology* 11, no. 1 (1997): 117-27.

Wallace, Patricia M. *The Psychology of the Internet.* Cambridge: Cambridge University Press, 1999.

Ward, Melanie, and David Newlands. "Use of the Web in Undergraduate Teaching." *Computers and Education* 31, no. 2 (1998): 171-84.

Washington State Department of Information Services. *Advancing the Digital State: The 1999 Washington State Information Technology Performance Report.* Olympia: Washington State Department of Information Services, 1999.

Watters, Carolyn, and Michael A. Sheperd. "Shifting the Information Paradigm from Data-Centered to User-Centered." *Information Processing and Management* 30, no. 4 (1994): 455-71.

Weber, Karen, and Wesley S. Roehl. "Profiling People Searching for and Purchasing Travel Products on the World Wide Web." *Journal of Travel Research* 37, no. 3 (1999): 291-98.

Wee, S. H. "Internet Use amongst Secondary School Students in Kuala Lumpur, Malaysia." *Malaysian Journal of Library and Information Science* 4, no. 2 (1999): 1-20.

Wersig, G. "The Problematic Situation as a Basic Concept of Information Science in the Framework of the Social Sciences: A Reply to Belkin." In *International Federation for Documentation: Theoretical Problems of Informatics,* 48-57. Moscow: VINITI, 1979.

Wiesenmayer, Randall L., and George R. Meadows. "Addressing Science Teachers' Initial Perceptions of the Classroom Uses of Internet and World Wide Web-Based Resource Materials." *Journal of Science Education and Technology* 6, no. 4 (1997): 329-35.

Wildemuth, Barbara M., and Ann L. O'Neill. "Research Notes: The 'Known' in Known-Item Searches: Empirical Support for User-Centered Design." *College and Research Libraries* 56 (1995): 265-81.

Wilhelm, Anthony G. *Democracy in the Digital Age: Challenges to Political Life in Cyberspace.* New York: Routledge, 2000.

Williams, Peter. "The Net Generation: The Experiences, Attitudes, and Behaviour of Children Using the Internet for Their Own Purposes." *ASLIB Proceedings* 51, no. 9 (1999): 315-22.

———. "Use of the Internet: Journalists: Not True to Type?" *Library Association Record* 100, no. 2 (1998): 84-85.

Williams, Raymond. *Marxism and Literature.* Oxford: Oxford University Press, 1977.

Wilson, Lizabeth A. "Building the User-Centered Library." *RQ* 34, no. 3 (1995): 297-302.

Wilson, T. D. "The Cognitive Approach to Information-Seeking Behavior and Information Use." *Social Science Information Studies* 4 (1984): 197-204.

Windham, Laurie, and Jon Samsel. *Dead Ahead: The Web Dilemma and the New Rules of Business.* New York: Allworth Press, 1999.

Winston, Brian. *Media Technology and Society: A History: From the Telegraph to the Internet.* London: Routledge, 1998.

Wolf, Alecia. "Exposing the Great Equalizer: Demythologizing Internet Equity." In *Cyberghetto or Cybertopia? Race, Class, and Gender on the Internet*, edited by Bosah L. Ebo, 15-32. Westport, Conn.: Praeger, 1998.

Wyman, S. K., C. R. McClure, J. B. Beachboard, and K. R. Eschenfelder. "Developing System-Based and User-Based Criteria for Assessing Federal Web Sites." Paper presented at the 60th Annual Meeting of the American Society for Information Science, 1997.

Yerbury, Hilary, and Joan Parker. "Novice Searchers' Use of Familiar Structures in Searching Bibliographic Information Retrieval Systems." *Journal of Information Science* 24, no. 4 (1998): 207-14.

Young, Gray, ed. *The Internet: The References Shelf.* New York: H. W. Wilson, 1998.

Young, Jeffrey S. *Forbes Greatest Technology Stories: Inspiring Tales of the Entrepreneurs and Inventors Who Revolutionized Modern Business.* New York: John Wiley & Sons, 1998.

Zakon, Robert H. "Hobbes' Internet Timeline V5.0." http://www. zakon.org/robert/internet/timeline/, 2000 [accessed 17 March 2000].

Zhang, Yin. "Scholarly Use of Internet-Based Electronic Resources: A Survey Report." *Library Trends* 47, no. 4 (1999): 746-70.

Index

academic community, vii, 9,
10, 15, 21, 53, 70-86, 177
access to technology, 6, 72-73,
86-87, 89, 93, 102, 104,
107-8, 129, 168, 178
administrative work, 75-77
adult education, 43
Advanced Research Projects
Agency (ARPA), 4-9, 32,
70
age and Internet use, 90, 95,
103, 117, 121, 125
American Psychological
Association (APA), 39-42
amplification, 57, 59, 157-159,
183. *See also* Latour,
Bruno
andragogy, 43
Andreessen, Marc, 10-11
ARPANET, 6-9, 160
attitudes toward the Internet,
99-101, 105, 107, 111-12,
120-21, 122-23, 165
Australia, 74, 115
Australian Academic and
Research Network
(AARNet), vii, 9, 33-34
authentic learning, 39-43

barriers, 48, 106-7, 109, 126,
128-29, 168
Belkin, Nicholas, 52
Berners-Lee, Tim, 10-11
Bina, Eric, 10-11
Boa Vista, 57, 60. *See also*
Latour, Bruno
browsers, 10-12, 81
businesses, 11-12, 15, 160. *See
also* e-commerce
business management, 36-37

Canada, 74, 87, 125, 127-28
catalogs, 88-89
Cerf, Vinton, 8, 14
CERN, 10
children, 107-12
circulating reference, 59-60
cognitive engineering, 44
cognitive viewpoint, 51-52
collaboration and Internet use,
90, 162
communication, 77-79, 91, 97,
110, 126-27, 160
computer experience and
Internet use, 73, 84, 90,
103, 123
computer networks. *See*
internetworking

215

About the Author

Harry Bruce is the Associate Dean for Research at the Information School of the University of Washington. He has been actively involved in researching information behavior and uses of the Internet for the past ten years. His research has been funded by competitive grants in Australia and the United States and is published in a wide range of national and international refereed journals. His Ph.D. thesis entitled "A user oriented view of the Internet as information infrastructure" was awarded the highly prestigious UMI Doctoral Dissertation Award by the American Society for Information Science and Technology.